BOOK B.

MW01256713

ADVANCED
STRATEGIES FOR INDIE AUTHORS

SELF-PUBLISHING GUIDE BOOK TWO

Robert J. Ryan

Cover design by 187designz

ISBN: 9781700403360
(print edition)

Trotting Fox Press

Contents

Introduction

Book blurbs. Book descriptions. Book jacket copy. Call it what you will, few things do more to sell a book – and few things are harder to write.

Nor does it help that everyone has an opinion on how to do it, and what works and what doesn't. Worse, those opinions rarely match.

Of course, you can study bestselling books to see what sort of blurbs they have. But some advisers say that's futile. These authors get where they are because of their name or their advertising budget. Copying them is a recipe for disaster.

Are these advisers right, though?

Perhaps some simple formula can be followed. Google "blurb writing formula" and quite a lot show up. They'll tell you how to create a masterpiece in seven easy steps. Or how to draft a perfect blurb … or a sizzling blurb that sells … or an irresistible blurb. Well, you get my drift.

The only thing is, the advice is still contradictory. And much of it comes from editors, who know a lot about the passive voice but little about marketing. Or it comes from writers, who may or may not understand marketing.

Who is to be believed? What formula should be followed? Is there a formula at all?

This book will answer those questions, and many more.

My aim is to provide detailed and actionable information on every aspect of blurb writing, from start to finish. I'll back up what I say, and nothing will be mere personal preference. I'll give you a resource that leaves no stone unturned in the quest for a great blurb. In short, my goal is to give you the *definitive* guide.

Truly, a great blurb is within reach of any writer. So too the better sales it will bring. All that's required is the right knowhow. I say this because all the blurb rewrites, and all the hard work in the world, isn't enough. The labor must be guided by correct knowledge, or the effort is lost.

When you finish this book, please tell me if I've given you that knowledge.

Who am I to Give Blurb Advice?

It's a good question. It's *the* question. Here's my answer.

Before I quit my job in March 2018 to become a full-time author, I worked for the government. Try not to hold a grudge against me. What I did there revolved around ensuring people complied with legislative requirements.

Worse, they were *tax* requirements.

Still holding that grudge at bay?

My core task back then was ensuring people complied with legislation … and often people would rather *not*. This is a problem all governments face, and not just for tax. As a result, they employ teams of people with copywriting, behavioral economics, behavioral insight and marketing skillsets. Their brief? Persuade people to do the right thing. Or at least what the legislation says is the right thing…

I was one of them. I was a persuader.

You might be surprised how seriously some government departments take this. They do so because in their world things are done on scale. Sending out a letter? That's not a walk down to the local post office. A single mail out might be fifty thousand at a time. All of a sudden, a letter that gets a 1% improvement in response rate saves the government a fortune in administrative expenses. It means fewer follow-up letters. It means fewer phone calls. And more people understanding and meeting their obligations. Governments just love that.

My department took it so seriously that we had access to regular focus groups, a support network across interstate and multijurisdictional lines and novelties like infrared eye-tracking technology. This technology allows research into how people read a web page, how they read a letter and what they look at and don't look at. We used every tool at our disposal to monitor what worked, and what didn't.

That's what I did. And I specialized in copywriting techniques. Others I worked with included behavioral psychologists, qualitative market research scientists and behavioral economists. We learned off each other and pooled our skills together to get the job done.

My work covered a wide field. Letters. Websites. Strategic advice on communication methods. Drafting ads for industry journals. Advising on training methods. Providing lectures to staff on the basic principles of copywriting. Heading a video project and drafting the script for it. Interesting stuff (but not as much fun as writing fiction).

Not long before I left, I won the department's inaugural innovation challenge. And (you guessed it) that was off the back of a copywriting concept.

Okay. I've risked boring you with this government stuff for a reason. Everything I was doing for my day job was fertile training for my next job – transforming myself from a part-time to a full-time indie publisher.

Now that's a job I don't have to apologize for.

My fiction is published under a pen name as well as my real name – Robert Ryan. For nonfiction, I insert a J.

And what have I achieved as an indie author? Long story short: freedom. I work for myself. I'm my own boss, and I earn a comfortable living. Comfortable enough that part of my writing schedule involves a post-lunch nana nap. Something that none of my copywriting skills ever convinced a government boss to approve. Go figure.

Now, your goals may not be the same as mine. If not, I urge you to at least consider the nana nap. But whatever they are, I'm pretty sure they involve finding ways to take your fiction-writing craft and infuse it with publishing expertise and marketing savvy so you can break out and reach the next level.

It can be done. I've done it. Blurbs are a critical factor in the process. In short, I know what you want to know, and the rest of this book provides that knowledge.

1. The True Purpose of a Blurb

You'll have heard that the purpose of the blurb is to sell the book. At best, that's an oversimplification. At worst, it's an error.

The blurb serves a function in the sales funnel. It's a component, and one of several, that act like cogs in a machine to get a job done. Other cogs, such as the cover, reviews and preview all serve their function as well.

But this is not a haphazard collection of cogs spinning and grinding at random. Like a Swiss watch, each cog works in harmony and turns at the exact right moment to produce the desired result.

And what's the desired result? To move the prospective buyer further along the sales funnel. If all goes well, when they reach the *end*, they'll buy.

This is the sales funnel:

Awareness of the product
Evaluation of the product
Interest is stimulated
Interest transforms into desire
Action occurs (buy or don't buy)

This is the process buyers go through to purchase a product. Don't take my word for it. Don't take anyone's word for anything. Always look for verification. Google is your friend.

Sometimes simple logic works well too. People don't buy a product, and then become aware of it. That's out of order, and the order of the sales funnel is well established, studied and utilized to great effect by marketers.

So, it's easy to see where the cover fits into the funnel. It sits at the top. Its function is to draw awareness to the book.

What do most prospective buyers (I'll use the marketing term of prospect from now on) do after clicking the cover? They read the blurb.

How do we know this? Because the blurb is where a cover click takes them. Amazon has billions and billions of data points about customer behavior on which to base website design. If their data showed that most people skipped the blurb and went straight to, say, the reviews, the cover click would take them to the reviews instead, and they would be at the top of the product page rather than the blurb.

After reading the blurb, the prospect has several options. Among them, that their interest isn't piqued and they click on an also-bought or an ad. In that case, they've left your sales funnel and moved into someone else's. This happens a lot, and it's the main reason blurbs are critically important. But for our current purpose, let's assume the prospect is still with us.

What do they do next? Moving back up to the top and clicking the buy button is certainly a possibility. No doubt some people will do just that. But those numbers aren't statistically relevant. We know, statistically, from marketing studies on digital platforms that reviews play a massive role in the sales funnel. They show the purchase decision is influenced anywhere from 80% to 98% of the time by reviews.

What does this tell us? It tells us that the prospect is *still in the evaluation phase* at the end of the blurb. Interest and desire may have built, but the buy point has *not* been reached. They're still looking for more data to inform their final decision.

If the blurb does its job, the prospect will move down to the reviews. Or maybe up to the preview. Probably both, although in what order is impossible to tell for certain.

So the purpose of the blurb is not to sell the book. Its use is to deepen interest and desire. Its marketing purpose is to move the prospect farther toward the end of the sales funnel. When they finally reach that point, that's where the buy or don't buy decision will be made.

Given the above, an overt "buy" call to action (CTA) at the end of the blurb, which some advisers recommend, is wrong. This is one of the reasons it annoys people. They're not *ready* to buy at that point. A buy CTA should only be deployed at the point where the buy/not buy decision is actually made. Another reason book buyers don't like it is that they aren't accustomed to the hard sell of a buy CTA in a blurb. It's not normal practice in blurbs, and it draws their attention and stands out to them as an attempt at marketing manipulation, and nobody responds well to being manipulated.

That the blurb is not the end point of the sales funnel doesn't diminish its influence. The blurb stimulates interest and desire, without which no sale will ever occur. But even with interest and desire, if the reviews are bad, then most prospects will baulk at buying. So too if they read the preview and the author's style doesn't resonate with them. In short, the blurb does the heavy lifting, but the reviews and preview seal the deal.

We can speculate that the preview is where the real buying action happens. Amazon puts a "Buy with 1-Click" CTA at the end of it. Notably, they could put the same CTA at the end of the blurb (or reviews) if they wanted to. But they don't.

So, what have we established?

Sentence by sentence, paragraph by paragraph, the blurb must strive to build interest until desire is kindled.

Then, the prospect will look at the reviews or preview. Desire is already high at this point, so this is a confirmation stage. It's not likely that good reviews will fan desire to a higher state, but bad reviews can certainly dampen things.

The preview is different. This is the greatest test of all. Will the story and author style resonate? If so, the buy CTA lies at its end.

Knowledge is power. And understanding where the blurb fits into the sales funnel allows us to choose the right wording to match the psychological state of the prospect, and drive more people to the reviews and preview.

Everything that follows in this book is about finding those right words.

2. Why Taglines Work

A book blurb, for all its brevity, is a complex piece of writing. It's made of separate components, each with a distinct function. We'll deal with these parts in turn, starting with the tagline.

The tagline is the first thing the reader sees. And first impressions count. We all know that, but in scientific terms the concept goes by the name of the halo effect, and marketers generally succeed or fail off this one concept. That's how important it is.

What happens is this. The human brain is wired to make decisions off limited data. It uses cues, or if you prefer scientific terms, heuristic decision-making tools such as rules of thumb, to make snap judgements.

And those snap judgements carry a disproportionately higher weight than they should. This is called anchoring, and the end result is that what the prospect sees first carries through with them the rest of the way and colors their judgement.

Or, if that snap judgment indicates no value, the prospect won't even bother to investigate further. On Amazon, that means clicking to someone else's book.

Like I said. First impressions count…

The tagline serves a similar function in a blurb that a headline does in a newspaper or the subject line of a marketing email. This is to attract the reader's eye, their attention and to signal that what follows will be worth their time. Its purpose is to get the person to continue reading.

To an extent, the blurb has the prospect's attention. After all, that's why they clicked on the cover. But the moment they get to the product page, there are a myriad of other things to distract their eye, such as a banner ad for someone else's book at the top of the page.

You want their gaze to go to your tagline, to the opening of your sales funnel rather than someone else's. How can you achieve this?

The method copywriters use is to make the text stand out. They use italics or bold. Sometimes they'll use larger fonts, or all capitals. They might also use eye-catching symbols such as asterisks or dollar signs.

Having said that, true copywriting professionals always know their target audience and adapt the general methods to the specific situation. So, for book buyers on Amazon, I'd shy away from gimmicky tricks such as large fonts. You see it now and then, but by its rarity it stands out that bit too much and calls attention to itself as deliberate manipulation. It might draw the gaze of a prospect in the first instance, but then it risks repelling them in the second.

For most genres, most of the time, stick to bold or italics. It'll get the job done nicely, and without risk of the prospect becoming wary.

How else can you draw the eye? In copywriting, it's the things you leave out that sometimes have the strongest effect. In this case, what you want to leave out is words. If the tagline is surrounded by whitespace, it'll pop. In color terms, it's a black foreground against a white background, which is the highest contrast you can get.

This isn't an unbreakable rule. It's just a reason to strive for a short, pithy tagline. But sometimes the best tagline isn't short and pithy. So be it. Content counts too. Content counts a lot. So much so that a long opening can convert better than a short one. More on the myth of the eight word or less opening later.

This leads to the next step. It's all well and good to draw the eye, but if the reader doesn't like what they're seeing it's to no purpose. So, what should a tagline actually say?

So many options. So many choices. So many possibilities. But one factor cuts through, and when you understand that then your focus becomes razor sharp.

That factor is attention span. It's often said that goldfish have an attention span of nine seconds. By comparison, humans had a digital attention span in the year 2000 of twelve seconds. Now, it's supposed to be eight seconds. It's dropping, and fast.

Of course, all studies and statistics are questionable. I don't think anyone can put an exact figure on this, still less how it applies to the specific situation of shopping for books on Amazon.

But the exact number of seconds doesn't matter. What matters is that attention spans are really, really short. If you haven't convinced someone in a matter of moments to keep reading, they likely won't.

Back to the burning question. What should a tagline say to hold attention and convince the prospect to read on?

To do this, as always with marketing, you have to think from the prospect's point of view. In this case, when you do that, you realize they clicked on the cover for a reason. That reason is *genre*.

When you browse the Amazon store, you'll see a lot of good covers. It doesn't matter if it's romance, westerns, thrillers or whatever. There are lots of good covers out there. But no matter how good the cover, no matter how well it signals genre, if you don't read romance books you're not going to click through to the blurb, regardless of how good the cover is. You're not *interested* in that type of book.

But if you do like romance, and you do click on the cover, what's going to keep your attention? The same thing that brought you there in the first place. Romance. That's what you're interested in reading, and if the content of the tagline signals it, you're much more likely to dive in than if the content doesn't signal it.

The point here is that just as a cover should signal genre, so too should the tagline. This is probably the most important element to get right. The best way to hold someone's attention is to give them what they're looking for. Failure to signal genre with the tagline is a critical error.

What else can you do with a tagline? This is another key to making them work. Never rely on just one thing. Good taglines are always multifaceted. So genre should be backed up with some kind of hook. There are many, many types of hook. So many that I devote the next chapter to them. But in short, a hook might be a teaser (what's known in marketing as an open loop) or it might be something startling. Or it might be poetic. Or it might trigger an emotional response. It should be several of these things at once if you can manage it. The more you do that, the more powerful it will be.

The best way to learn this is to look at an example, and then deconstruct it. This is the tagline to Mark Dawson's *The Cleaner*.

MI6 created him. Now they want him dead.

This is a simple tagline, but effective. It makes good use of the contrast between black text and whitespace. MI6 is a powerful element. Those three characters conjure an array of story possibilities and genre. We immediately think spies, James Bond, thrills and adventure. Those three small characters act like a needle shooting adrenaline into our veins. At least if you like spy thrillers. That's also what the very start of the tagline does. It announces the genre loud and clear.

But what else is going on? Is there another layer to the tagline beside offering a subject of high interest to the prospect?

Yes there is. There are also two open loop style hooks. *MI6 created him.* What does that mean? What exactly is he? A spy? An assassin? Something else? The only way to find out is to keep reading. The second open loop is stronger. *Now they want him dead.* Again, why? Has he done something to trigger that? Does he know something he shouldn't?

Already, by signaling genre so strongly, this is a good tagline. The open loops intensify that. But there's more. The tagline pulls readers in on an emotional level. The reader feels a sense of sympathy. MI6 created this person, now they want him dead? That's betrayal. Whoever this guy is, we've already taken his side.

It's a short tagline, but it achieves a lot. It does so because it's working in layers. The same words carry multiple levels of meaning. A tagline that does this will draw prospects forward. It has their attention.

This leads to my final comment on taglines. It's often said that a good tagline should encapsulate the whole story. This is an error.

I believe the people who advocate this are taking the practice of loglines used to describe films and applying it to books. But a logline for a movie operates more as a mini synopsis than a hook with multiple layers. They're not the same thing.

The origin of loglines derives from Hollywood. Large studios that owned many scripts would keep a logbook that maintained very short summaries of what each script was about. The logline served a clerical function. Now, that mini-synopsis structure is maintained, but a hook may be added.

A tagline for a book blurb is a marketing tool designed and structured purely to attract attention. It's all hook (and in fact a copywriter would use that term in preference to ether logline or tagline), and it's most definitely not a mini synopsis.

3. Hooks are More than Teasers

Hooks are used in fiction. They're an ancient literary device. They're used in marketing too, and there are quite a few different types.

Most people think of a hook as some kind of teaser. In marketing, this is called an open loop. It's so named because the question being posed remains unanswered. Thus the "loop" isn't closed. Think of it as something like a joke that has all the hallmarks of being funny, but the punchline is delayed. You know it's coming though, and anticipation builds.

Open loops are powerful. But if that's the only type of hook a blurb has, it's swimming in the shallow end of the pool.

Let's run through the most common types of hook, with examples. First, the open loop.

Open loops

As said, the purpose of an open loop is to pose some kind of a question, either directly or indirectly, and then delay giving the answer. This can be very powerful. Its effect though, generally, is short-lived.

Have you ever watched a movie, and it's gone to an ad break on a cliffhanger? Ah, the pain! The anxiety! The state of mental torture! And yet, ad by ad, the tension dissipates like vapor into the air. By the time the movie starts again, your psychological state has changed. It's gone from OMG! to whatevs.

Such is the lifespan of most open hooks. Like a shooting star they appear and then vanish. If you want them to have a longer impact, you can do so by investing them with emotion. An open loop driven by deep emotion lasts longer than an open loop fueled by curiosity alone.

Here's a run of the mill example of an open loop.

SOMETIMES...DEAD IS BETTER

This is from the Kindle edition of Stephen King's *Pet Sematary*. For those wondering, King deliberately chose to spell cemetery incorrectly. This is how a sign, written by a child, appears in the book.

I'm not going to accuse Mr. King of marketing. I have a feeling he would hate that very much. But I'm sure that the marketing department of his publisher was happy with the choice of title. As you'll see shortly, this kind of thing is a potent hook in its own right.

Back to the open loop in the tagline. It's a strong one, because you really have to ask the question ... in what scenario is dead better? It also goes some way to establishing genre, which is horror. Perfect.

The fact

This is a classic copywriting hook. Its premise is pretty simple. You start with a fact, but not just any fact. Choose one that grabs the attention of the audience.

Katniss Everdeen lives in a future where people, even children, are forced to fight to the death. For TV entertainment.

Well, that's not from the real blurb for *The Hunger Games*. I made it up, but I think it's an improvement. (Yes, I know. I *would* say that).

This kind of hook is the opposite of an open loop. It merely states a fact, but in doing so it can achieve quite a few things. As in this example, it can introduce the main character in an interesting way. It engages prospect sympathy and emotion. Who wouldn't feel sorry for Katniss? It gives us some world building, which in this case is also genre – dystopian post-apocalyptic. And it offers some pretty sharp contrast (yet another type of hook) in the fight to the death and TV entertainment business.

"The fact" is one of the best copywriting hooks going around. Even better for book blurbs because it's not used often by writers. They're generally unaware of copywriting tactics, and this rarity enhances its impact.

The statement

Almost the same as "the fact", but not quite. The statement doesn't have to be true. It could just be what the character thinks. It needn't relate to world building or setting. It's just a statement of some thought or situation. Think of it like a newspaper headline. Its job is to attract attention by giving information rather than withholding it. By giving information, it signals genre and foreshadows story elements.

Husband and wife treasure-hunting team Sam and Remi Fargo ARE BACK in a brand-new thrilling adventure to find an ancient scroll which carries a deadly curse...

This is the tagline to Clive Cussler's *The Oracle*. It tells us in a pretty straightforward way who the heroes are and what they're searching for. There's an open loop at the end, though not an especially strong one. Most of its force comes from the ellipsis, which suggests more is to happen that hasn't been said.

For the most part, this hook isn't trying to whip up curiosity levels by open loops. It's telling the prospect that another book in this series is out. This iteration happens to be number 11. This is why "ARE BACK" is capitalized, which is a classic copywriting technique. It's drawing attention to the fact that this is a new book in an old series, and the tagline is telling us who is doing what. Other simple statements establish genre: treasure-hunting team and thrilling adventure.

In short, it's the kind of hook that many writers or blurb advisers would say "is giving away too much of the plot and it needs a stronger hook."

But copywriters always target an audience. This is book eleven of the series, and the audience is mostly people who have read previous books. What's going to interest them most? The characters they've loved from previous books doing genre-related things.

This isn't to say that a statement type hook can't work for book one of a series too. It can, and very effectively.

The say whaaat?

This hook operates by causing startlement. When the human mind is surprised, attention focuses like a laser on the object that caused the surprise. This is a biological survival mechanism, and copywriters use it to great effect. Like most hooks, its usefulness is short-lived. That's okay. A book blurb isn't meant to be *War and Peace*.

Pet Sematary, discussed above, garners attention by the deliberate spelling error. *Tomorrow, When the War Began* is another book title that operates similarly. It messes with your sense of time in the way that "Sematary" messes with your spelling instincts.

I was dead when they offered me the mission. I accepted it anyway.

Another made up one. (I love creating taglines and writing blurbs.) This attracts attention by its apparent bending of reality and its nonchalant acceptance of that strange reality. It also serves up a few open loops, but it's a bit weak in terms of genre. Still, it hints well enough at urban fantasy, I think.

Be careful of employing this type of hook. You don't want to pull a bait and switch tactic. The rest of the blurb, and the book itself, have to live up to it. If not, you've created clickbait rather than a hook. And that'll hurt you in the long run.

The poetic hook

This can be very tricky. It's not a hook for the fainthearted, because it can backfire easily. But using rhyme and other poetic devices can attract the eye and focus attention.

Other poetic devices? I'm thinking chiefly of alliteration and iambic meter here.

Whoever wins ... we lose.

This is the tagline (not logline) from the *Alien vs. Predator* movie. As most good taglines do, it has a few things going for it at the same time. First up, it has alliteration. It also has consonance. But most of all, it has a sense of contrast balanced on either side of the ellipsis. Winning. Losing.

These work, as all hooks do, by getting attention. Things that contrast stand out. It's an immensely powerful technique. Not just in copywriting, but in literature. Here are a few examples drawn from some of the most memorable literature ever written.

To be, or not to be? *Hamlet*, by William Shakespeare.

Fair is foul, and foul is fair. *Macbeth*, by William Shakespeare.

All for one, and one for all. *The Three Musketeers*, by Alexandre Dumas.

It was the best of times, it was the worst of times, it was the age of wisdom, it was the age of foolishness, it was the epoch of belief, it was the epoch of incredulity, it was the season of Light, it was the season of Darkness, it was the spring of hope, it was the winter of despair ... *A Tale of Two Cities*, by Charles Dickens.

As you can see, these operate on a poetic level too. There's iambic meter in each example, even the last. And there's also either alliteration or assonance. More than anything though, the power of antagonistic forces give these words life.

A far stretch to use this in a book blurb? Perhaps. But here's one I prepared earlier.

She was alive. He wanted her dead.

Not my best work, but not a bad tagline. It operates mostly by the contrast, but there's alliteration and iambic meter going on too.

The direct question

This is moderately common. It's a variation of the open loop, but it *directly* asks the reader a question. Psychologically, this tends to make the reader want to answer it. That's what you do when someone asks you a question, isn't it?

See what I did there? I thought you'd notice.

The power of the direct question is that it creates engagement. While the reader is thinking of the answer, they're not clicking away. Of course, the open loop part has to be strong too. Asking a question for which the answer is very obvious doesn't do much good. Try for a question that really makes the reader think.

Could you murder your wife to save your daughter?

That's the tagline for Adam Croft's *Her Last Tomorrow*. You can see that it's more than just an open loop. As that alone, it would go something like this. *A man faces a terrible dilemma. Murder his wife, or his child will be killed.*

The real tagline has more force because of the direct question. It also has contrast going on in a strong way. Someone has to die so someone else can live.

There you have it. These are a few types of hooks. It's not by any means a comprehensive list.

As always, don't take my word for any of this. Google something like "types of hooks in copywriting." Study what you find. I haven't gone into detail here because, frankly, just the subject of hooks alone could fill an entire book. My purpose here is to expand your horizons and give you a direction for research. Open loops really are just swimming in the shallow end of the pool. Copywriting is much deeper than this amateur level. The higher you raise yourself above amateur, the better you'll sell books in the massively competitive world that is indie publishing.

The thing to keep in mind is that there are many, many types of hook. But the key is that they *all* work best when they're multilayered. A multilayered hook is a super-hook. Achieve that, and you're well on your way to blurbs that convert better than your competition.

4. Alternative Blurb Openings

Taglines are beautiful things. And effective. As a marketer, they make my heart sing because they do so much with so few words. But they're not the only way to open a blurb. Nor are they necessarily the best.

Here, we'll explore the alternatives and discuss their pros and cons. The thing to keep in mind is that you have choices. There are lots of ways to open a blurb. As with anything else, it's usually not a case of method A is better than method B, or C etc. It's a case of understanding the technique properly, whichever is chosen, and executing it *well*.

The story quote

It's not that uncommon to start with a quote direct from the book itself. Traditional publishers do it far more than indies do. There's no good reason for that.

There's a theory that a quote followed by "normal" blurb matter might cause confusion. Does this theory hold up?

No. Anything can cause confusion. Anything can be written clearly. As said above, it comes down to execution. Do it well, and it'll be a seamless transition from quote to the rest of the blurb.

"I am Johannes Verne, and I am not afraid."

This is the opening of the blurb for *The Lonesome Gods*, by Louis L'Amour. First, let's study the transition. The paragraph immediately below the quote starts with this. "This was the boy's mantra as he plodded through the desert alone, left to die by his vengeful grandfather."

Well, there's no confusion there. The transition is as smooth as George Clooney in a tuxedo. We can lay the confusion myth to rest.

What else is going on? The quote's acting exactly like a tagline. I don't just mean the formatting – italicized and surrounded by whitespace. I mean on a hook level. The very fact that he says he's not afraid is a nice, big, juicy open loop. Obviously, there *is* something to be afraid of. But what?

Time to dig a bit deeper. Is the open loop all that's going on? Not by a longshot. There's iambic meter as well. Not to mention assonance of both stressed vowels and identical consonants. Also, count the syllables. There are six to each half of the sentence, divided by the comma. This is poetry under the guise of prose. It's not overt, but it's there. And it gives the sentence gravitas and beauty. Just the thing to provide a bit more zest to the open loop.

So, what have we learned? Quotes are a great way to start a blurb, so long as you avoid confusion. And, in effect, they operate exactly like a tagline. That is, you can use any of the hooks, or better yet, a multiple layer of hooks, just the same as a tagline.

In the example, there's something else too. The first sentence of the blurb itself builds directly off the quote. And it induces emotion. In this case, sympathy. Think of these words. *Plodded through the desert. Alone. Left to die. Vengeful grandfather.*

The review quote

Another favorite of traditional publishing. Sometimes used by indies, but there's far more scope for it.

There's one pivotal question to ask if you're considering this tactic. Is everyone's opinion of equal value?

The answer to that is no. Blurbs aren't a democracy where everyone has an equal voice. Some voices are more worthy than others. Some will sell better than others.

First, let's consider where you might get such a quote, and then we'll rank them by how great their influence is over prospects.

Quotes from some sort of literary expert are common enough in traditional publishing. These generally come from a newspaper column or some such. Similar are quotes from a fellow author, especially one who has gained a following of their own. Next comes a quote from a well-known blog or online magazine. Then, lastly, quotes from actual readers taken from a place such as Goodreads or Amazon. This last is something I've only ever seen done by indies.

Do any of these quote types work? Do some work better than others? What, if any, behavioral insight or marketing knowhow informs the tactic?

Well, there's a strong basis for the practice. It's called social proof. When in doubt, and the choice of whether to buy or not to buy, or even to like or not to like, *always* creates doubt, people utilize information gathering techniques to help them decide. One of these is what other people think.

Humans are amazingly social. In animals, it's called herd behavior. People will often say things such as, "I think for myself." Or, "Marketing has no influence on me." It's not my place to doubt them. But good marketing operates at an unconscious level. The desire to conform, and the desire to belong to a group, and the desire to seek the opinions of others are strong instincts. Much more of what people do in their everyday lives is influenced by instinct than they think. Possibly *most* of what they do is influenced by unconscious factors.

This is another way of saying social proof is a powerful thing. But not all social proof is equal. Generally, people are more influenced by people they relate to. In particular, people are more inclined to be persuaded by their "equals" than their "superiors". Google social proof on a site like Wikipedia for evidence.

What does this mean for review quotes? It means quotes from the literary establishment are likely less influential than quotes from everyday readers. I'll take a stab in the dark and say that surprised you.

A lot of marketing and behavioral insights are like that. This is why knowledge is power. This is how you get an edge on your competitors.

So, I wouldn't use a quote from some sort of literary institution. At least I'd hesitate, no matter how good it sounded.

Indies aren't likely to get such a quote anyway, although some do pay for things like Kirkus reviews. I suggest you spend the hundreds of dollars involved on a better cover. Or keep that money safely in your bank account. The same applies to online blogs and magazines. Their quotes are less likely to resonate with readers and influence their opinion.

Real quotes from real readers can work a treat. If you can, attach a name to it rather than "Amazon reviewer" although that may not always be possible. If not, don't worry about it. But the name adds to the feeling that it's genuine, and it contributes to the sense of the review coming from a person the prospect "can relate to" and that is their "equal". This is done frequently, but I have to point out that Amazon might not approve of using a reviewer's name.

What about other writers? This is trickier. Is a quote from a writer coming from a superior or an equal? I would say that a writer is *not* considered part of the establishment or a superior. I think they're considered equals, but ones with specific subject matter expertise. They're authorities rather than superiors. This, theoretically, puts them at the top of the pile in terms of review quotes.

What about in reality? We know that traditional publishing uses the tactic, and they use it frequently. That's a good sign. Despite what some advisers say, publishing houses with multi-million-dollar marketing departments actually know a thing or two about marketing.

But we also have BookBub. They split test their blurbs and provide a lot of results in their blog. This is a goldmine of information, and I suggest you check it out. Bear in mind though that what works on BookBub customers, in a BookBub email, isn't necessarily the same as what works best on a retail site such as Amazon. Still, it's a good guide.

Their research showed that including a quote from a well-known author in the genre increased the average click-through rate by 30.4%. When figures for quotes from authors and publications were combined, the click-through rate only increased by 22.6%. Publication quotes were dragging the author quotes down, badly.

This is not to say that some sort of a publication quote doesn't help, but its influence is minimal. I would much, much rather go with a good tagline than a quote from a publication any day of the week.

Here's how the pros do it. If you've networked with a bestselling indie author, you just might be able to do the same thing. Here's the opening to *Thin Air*, by Lisa Gray. The rest of the blurb is a masterclass in blurb writing too.

"Lisa Gray explodes onto the literary stage, with this taut, edge-of-your-seat thriller, and her headstrong protagonist, Jessica Shaw, reminiscent of Lee Child's Jack Reacher, delivers a serious punch." —Robert Dugoni, *New York Times* bestselling author.

That's pro marketing, boys and girls. Shall we count the ways I love it? First, as discussed, it's a quote from a bestselling author. But we want more than that. We want layers of other hooks.

We have them. It's a thriller, and the language signals genre. *Explodes. Taut. Edge-of-your-seat. Thriller.* It introduces the main character, and gives us a reason to like them. *Headstrong.* Readers don't like wishy-washy and weak characters. It also foreshadows there'll be conflict ahead, which is an open loop. Then we have a reference to a similar author in Lee Child. Also a powerful tool to sell. See the BookBub research for evidence of this.

That's a seriously good opening. If you're stuck on the concept that a blurb opening has to be an open loop, you may not see it. But prospects haven't been taught the myth that only open loops work. They don't even know what an open loop is. But they do know if a blurb *interests* them.

Awards. Accolades. Bestseller status

I group these together because of their similarity. They're commonly used to open blurbs, among both traditional publishers and indies.

Again, social proof is at work. But as we discovered above, not all social proof is equal. These have a weakness. No *person* is behind them, and they therefore have diminished power. People are much more influenced by other people than impersonal institutions or labels.

Yet that doesn't mean they have no power. BookBub testing showed mentioning an award increased click-through rate by 6.7%. This is only a slight improvement compared to author quotes at 30.4%, and mentioning comparable titles at 25.7%. But another test they did showed awards could boost click through by up to 25%, but on average the increase was only 5%.

I would suggest you would need a very well known, and a very prestigious award, to register at the higher end of the spectrum.

This type of opening also has another weakness. It's pretty much impossible to layer it with other hooks. Linking to genre can be done, but that's about it.

So, use this tactic sparingly. Use it if you have an awesome accolade. And I mean truly awesome. Otherwise, one of the other options is likely to be a better bet.

The standard sentence or paragraph

You don't have to use a fancy schmancy tagline or some such. Lots of people don't. There's no rule against a standard sentence or even paragraph. The copywriting tactics of white space, bold or italics are just that. Tactics. They're useful, but dispensable.

Strategies are stronger. Strategies are the driving force and tactics just the handiest means available at the time. And the strategy of any blurb opening is to attract attention, and overlay that with hooks that propel the prospect further along the sales funnel.

A sentence can do that without being a tagline. So too a paragraph. This is the opening of the blurb for *The Vagrant*, by Peter Newman.

The Vagrant is his name. He has no other.

Years have passed since humanity's destruction emerged from the Breach.

Friendless and alone he walks across a desolate, war-torn landscape.

There's no bold or italics, just a simple dive straight into the blurb. Simple is the operative word. The sentences are short, and whitespace is used well. This is important, because the second sentence of the blurb verges on confusing. It's a bit hard to know what to make of it. But it's an open loop, if a risky one. Yet the simplicity before and after helps it through.

Also, we have a liberal dose of sympathy again. He doesn't have a name. Humanity's destruction. Friendless and alone.

Referencing other authors

Another popular technique. But this one has a bad name. How is that possible? Can something be popular, and yet have a bad name at the same time?

Obviously, it can. There are two groups. Those who use the tactic because they know it works. And those who listen to advice on Internet forums about how to sell books from people who aren't selling books.

Ouch! That was a bit rough. Nevertheless, true.

There's a reason it has a bad name, but it comes down to execution. Use the tactic well, and it can work; use it badly, and it might backfire.

Comparing to a famous author in terms of quality is a mistake. Referencing to establish similarity, especially with some sort of twist, helps the prospect learn *exactly* what kind of book they're looking at. And it does so with incredible conciseness. This brevity is worth its weight in gold.

Game of Thrones meets _Gladiator_ in this debut epic fantasy about a world caught in an eternal war, and the young man who will become his people's only hope for survival.

This is the opening to _The Rage of Dragons_, by Evan Winter. At least it's the opening for the hardback edition. The Kindle edition is different.

It's a statement style opening. It tells us exactly what the book is. And the chief contributor to this is referencing other works. But it doesn't _compare_ itself to them in quality terms.

BookBub has something to say on the subject as well. Their split testing shows mentioning comparable works increased click through by 25.7%.

A word of warning though. Statistics never lie. Except when they do. The BookBub platform is _not_ Amazon. Specifically, their buying demographic is different. It's skewed toward women, people of a somewhat older age group and certain genres.

In particular, BookBub buyers trust the BookBub curation process, and they're looking for a quick buy recommended to them by BookBub rather than the long slog of researching on Amazon themselves. This means they're more likely to pay attention to snippets of information that tell them a lot in a hurry. So, bear this in mind. The referencing technique is effective, but it'll be _far_ less effective on Amazon than BookBub.

All in all, the above is a pretty comprehensive list of blurb opening possibilities. Each of them is also open to variation. You have a lot to choose from, and I hope I've opened your mind to new possibilities and given you a good idea how to use them.

But let one key concept guide you in your decision-making process.

Choose the *best* opening you have for your particular book. Create different ones, and pick the strongest. Look for an opening that signals genre and is overlaid with multiple hooks. It'll serve you well.

And it better. Pretty much everything depends on it, so don't skimp on time and effort to come up with the best you can.

5. Above the Fold: Tips and Pitfalls

Did you think we were finished with the blurb opening? I mentioned in the introduction that I wasn't going to leave any stone unturned in the search for a brilliant blurb. So there's one more critical element to discuss before we move on to the next phase of the sales funnel.

As always when writing sales copy, you have to put yourself in the shoes of the prospect. What's in it for them? What do they want? What kind of experience are they having reading it? What forces are at play that might stop them from reading?

For blurbs on Amazon, there's one vital force at play. It's the "Read more" call to action. This CTA allows a blurb snippet above it of five lines when viewed on a PC. Fewer if you use a large font, which as discussed earlier is likely a mistake. This is another mark against it. And fewer lines of text if you have paragraph spacing, which you will. Otherwise, the first thing the prospect will see is an unappealing chunk of text like a brick.

But the click itself is the worst of it. The moment sales copy has a click, prospects drop off like marathon runners ascending a hill at the end of the race.

Why does Amazon do this? Why do they make it hard for someone to read the rest, and probably the bulk, of your blurb?

Amazon doesn't do much without a reason. The way they structure their website reflects billions of data points showing customer behavior. If most customers read the blurb, you can bet Amazon would display it in full. They give customers what they want. But their data shows them people don't read the blurb in full. Probably less than half do so. Maybe considerably less than half.

Amazon doesn't supply us with their statistics, but we can deduce a lot by their webpage design. We also know from marketing knowledge in general that the drop off for people reading a newspaper headline, email subject line, blog title etc. is *massive*.

This is why it's important to optimize the above the fold space. If you don't, your reader is gone. If you do, you've given them motivation to click "Read more". Without that click, you'll never get the buy click later.

This leads to the obvious question. How can that limited space above the fold be structured and optimized to earn the prospect's click?

Frontloading is the answer. Frontloading is used in marketing, journalism and webpage design to show the prospect or reader that what follows is of high interest to them. This is why the fact and statement type hook are so powerful. More powerful even than an open loop.

An open loop might drive curiosity, but if it's about subject matter that the prospect isn't interested in, it'll fall flat. You can charge your visitor's whiskey glass with rocket fuel, but that won't make them toast your health. On the other hand, if there's an open loop embedded in a fact or statement type hook – we have liftoff, Houston.

This reaffirms everything we discussed in previous chapters about the *content* of the opening. Frontload targeted information of high interest and embed it with other hooks. But another question remains. How best can we use the above the fold real estate *structurally*?

Should we utilize all five lines? After all, the more text above the fold the more opportunity to signal genre and dangle hooks. Not using that space is like a car salesperson taking a nana nap while a customer with questions wanders around the showroom floor.

Alternatively, if the salesperson comes over like your long-lost twin and shadows your every step blabbering away incessantly in your ear, it's too much. That's the equivalent of a wall of text in a blurb, and it's repellent.

The answer, as with so much else in life, is balance. Extremism in either direction is a fault that will cost you sales.

A wall of text, no matter how hooky it is, looks hard to read. Bearing in mind the halo effect discussed earlier, it will shade the prospect's judgement of the rest of the blurb. They'll be categorizing the blurb as chunky, complex and difficult to read. They'll probably think the book will be the same.

This genuine problem leads to some people writing a blurb opening like this:

The king was alone…

But that would not last…

…Soon the army would arrive.

This is the other extreme. I'm sure you've seen it about. It, too, is an error. Every bit as much as a wall of text.

Copywriters like to use simple text and lots and lots of whitespace. But this sort of thing is on the sparse side even for them. Generally, a copywriter would place a whole lot more than that above the fold. Even just the subject lines in a marketing email usually contain more words than that.

This is for a reason. You need a bit of space to move around in so you can convey subject matters of interest. You need space to move in order to embed layers of different types of hooks. Extremely short copy, especially just before a click in order to unfold the rest of the content, is asking for trouble.

Another way of looking at this is that a salesperson needs to talk enough to start selling the product, but not too much. It's about balance. Utilize the space Amazon gives you. Don't under use it. Whitespace makes the words look good, but it does nothing to sell a product. The words do that.

This is also noteworthy. Statistics show that 43% of American adults have basic or below basic literacy skills. This is why copywriting for general products, say an ad for shampoo aimed at a wide target audience, isn't written like a PhD thesis. But blurbs are written for *book readers*. They can handle a sentence or two. Even three or four.

The other trend evident in the made-up example above is the use of ellipses. An ellipsis is a beautiful thing in copywriting. It's powerful. But like anything good, don't overuse it. The more you use it the weaker its effect. Two is probably the most you would want to use in an entire blurb. Best results will come from spreading this out. For instance, one at the end of a tagline and one at the end of the blurb.

The overuse of ellipses also undermines the attempt to keep things looking clean and simple. All those dots make the whitespace look cluttered and dirty like a mess of breadcrumbs on a kitchen bench. They also have the effect of giving the prose a disjointed feel. In fact, this tactic usually *does* break apart words that would normally flow together. Separating the words is also delaying and diluting the impact of their meaning.

In the end, the tactic is at high risk of achieving the exact opposite of its intention. And, of course, by its unusualness it draws attention to itself as marketing. This also undermines it.

I have more to say on the best use of ellipses – and other copywriting-derived punctuation tricks soon...

6. How Blurbs Win the Dating Game

Seriously. Blurbs tease and seduce.

But after the initial eye-contact of the opening, they have to work to build a deeper connection. This phase of the blurb is to spark interest, and to keep sparking that interest.

Initial attraction isn't enough. Attraction is fleeting. Interest is needed to form a stronger bond. There's a getting-to-know-you period. Without this, you just have a sultry look across the room.

Okay. Enough of the romance talk. You get my drift now. Blurbs, like any sales copy, have to develop interest. They need to fulfill the promise of that first glance.

How do they do it?

They do it by being vulnerable and revealing something of themselves. They show their true self, not a fake mask designed to look appealing.

Sorry. I'm trying to stop the romance talk. I promise.

But that really hit the nail on the head. (Less of a romance-y analogy there, huh?) The way to develop interest is to keep giving the prospect what they want. If they clicked on a cover expecting to find epic fantasy, give them some slice or aspect of the book's plot that tallies up with that. Don't give them vague, non-genre material.

You don't want to provide the life story of the main character. You're after an element of plot that signals genre but that's also interesting. That element could come from the beginning of the book. Or the middle. Even, if you're careful, from near the end. You can do this because the golden rule of developing interest is that for every bit of information you give, you *pose more questions*.

Examples will follow to show this. The next step in the getting-to-know-you phase is to keep doing the same. You might take that initial glimpse into plot, and expand on it. You might introduce a second plot element. Or several plot elements.

Don't get carried away here. Don't introduce too much plot. You're not telling them the whole story, just a select aspect of the story. Exactly like you might tell a first date what kind of movies you like. You're not giving them a detailed analysis of your viewing habits since childhood.

There are a few other ingredients to throw into this mix. Flour is the basis of most cakes. But you also want a rising agent. In blurbs, this is conflict.

Introduce the prospect to some sort of conflict. It should be genre related. *Everything* in a blurb should be genre related. If it isn't, ditch it.

The conflict may be a glimpse of the overarching problem of the entire story. Or it could be subplot. Or both. Just keep it genre related and interesting.

Cakes are good. A nice fluffy sponge cake is marvelous. But it needs more to be edible than just a rising agent. It needs flavors. It needs sugar. It needs more ingredients.

What are the other ingredients a blurb needs?

There are two more that will make it near-irresistible. The first is a sense that the main character is likeable.

Just like on a date, a person who gushes about what a nice person they are is a turn off. Probably because we don't believe them. But a date who treats the waiter or waitress really well, or a stranger who happens to ask for directions, gets bonus points. They're *showing* they're nice people. Actions speak louder than words.

So, never tell the prospect your main character is likeable. Or funny. Or brave. Or anything else that's admirable and will induce people to like them. Slip a few words in the blurb that *show* it instead. Sometimes just the slightest change to wording can bring this out, and a hero to cheer for in a genre the prospect likes to read is a powerful combination.

Next, try to introduce a few pinches of emotion. Emotion, like cinnamon or ginger or nutmeg, is a potent spice. Just a little goes a long way.

Any emotion brings results. But it's particularly effective if its genre related. Loneliness in a character is good in romance. Fear works well in heroic fantasy. But these are the emotions of the character. You want this, but you want even more that the *prospect* feels emotion.

How does the prospect respond to the situation or emotion of the character? Usually with sympathy. At least, if you've worked to produce that effect. And it's something you should consider doing. It's something you should *really* consider because few things will ever work better for you when you get it right.

Of all the wide range of human emotion, sympathy is probably the strongest and quickest to manifest. We can feel intense sympathy for total strangers. It can happen instantaneously. What other emotion is like that?

The important point here is that we can feel sympathy for *strangers*. That's critical because a blurb is probably only three or four paragraphs long. The main character *is* a stranger.

We reserve other emotions, such as love or hate, for people we know. Sympathy circumvents all our safeguards and barriers. It strikes quick, and it hits strong. Get that going in your blurb, and your sales will go up.

Time for a few examples. The is the third and fourth paragraph from the Kindle-edition blurb for Dean Koontz's *Forever Odd.*

Odd Thomas, that unlikely hero, once more stands between us and our worst fears.

Odd never asked to communicate with the dead – they sought him out, in the small desert town of Pico Mundo, which he can never leave. He has already lost the love of his life; and now a childhood friend has disappeared and the worst is feared.

Those two paragraphs do a lot of work. Just like taglines and other openings can be layered, so too the rest of a blurb.

At an informational level, we learn a fair bit about this Odd Thomas character and his world. He can communicate with the dead. Something bad is happening. We know where he lives, and something of his personal life. And his childhood friend is missing. Not only is this giving us information, but it's also showing genre.

But as it's giving us all this information, it's posing questions at the same time. What exactly are our worst fears? What's going on in Pico Mundo? Why can he never leave? Why have the dead sought Odd out? What's happened to his friend?

On an emotional level, there's a lot going on too. Odd is an "unlikely" hero. This indicates he does his best, but he's not really a hero type. He's an underdog hero. This makes him likeable (as opposed to a brash hero).

We also learn that he never asked to communicate with the dead. This probably comes with a whole lot of trouble, and it's not something people would want. It invokes sympathy for him. He can't leave his home. This also invokes a degree of sympathy. Next, we discover he's lost the love of his life. Wow. This guy never gets a break. This is the *motherlode* of sympathy. But despite it all, he's trying to help. This paints him as likeable and admirable.

It's important to note that at no stage does Odd feel sympathy for himself. All these emotions and characterizations are being placed on him from "outside" so to speak. That makes them stronger and more believable.

Here's another example of the getting to know you stage. It's the fourth paragraph of the blurb for Duncan Hamilton's *The Wolf of the North*.

It has been generations since the Northlands have seen a hero worthy of the title. Many have made the claim, but few have lived to defend it. Timid, weak, and bullied, Wulfric is as unlikely a candidate as there could be.

I'll sift through this in layers again. Firstly, the book is epic fantasy, and here we're given some of the standard tropes of the genre. *Hero. Unlikely candidate.* Timid, weak and bullied isn't quite standard fare. But it's just a variation on the simple-farm-boy-becomes-a-king theme, which drips epic fantasy. Another trope of the genre is a "high style" voice. Read that paragraph of the blurb again. It's not normal style. It's elevated diction. It has a certain tight grandeur reminiscent of the best of classic epic fantasy.

The paragraph is giving us information about Wulfric, and the world in which he lives. But it poses more questions than it answers. Why do the Northlands need a hero? Why has it been so long since they've had one? How is it that someone timid, weak and bullied is a candidate for the job?

Once more, layered underneath everything, is a building sympathy for this Wulfric person. It comes from contrast. On the one hand, many people seem to try to be the hero, but die. On the other hand, Wulfric, despite his difficulties, is a candidate. Not to mention that he's bullied.

Time for one more. This is the third paragraph of the blurb for H.M. Ward's *The Arrangement Vol 1*.

FML is becoming Avery's motto. Just when she thinks things couldn't get any worse, they do. When her car stalls out at a busy intersection and she gets out to check under the hood, a guy steals her car. Armed with a dress and a pair of chucks, Avery runs after the thief. When a hot stranger offers to help, she can't say no. That's how Avery meets Sean Ferro, the totally sexy, totally damaged guy with more secrets than she has time for.

You know the pattern by now. Is this paragraph reinforcing genre? You bet. *Hot stranger. Totally sexy. Totally damaged.* These are some of the key tropes of New Adult Romance.

Is it revealing information but posing more questions as it does so? Yeppers. What's going on in Avery's life that her motto is FML? What happens to the car thief? What's going to happen with this Sean guy? What secrets does he have?

What about sympathy? Yep, we have that in bucket loads. Her motto is FML, so things aren't so good. Her car breaks down. Then it gets stolen. All in all, plenty of reason to feel a bit sorry for her. But she has spirit too. She chases after the car thief. So we like her. This is like salt on a steak or cream on a scone. It lifts things to a higher level.

So, all in all, this getting to know you stage of a blurb is incredibly useful. It builds on the attraction and awareness of the opening. It deepens emotion. It gives you more reason to care and reaffirms genre at every step. If it were a date, you'd know you'd found a connection with somebody, and you'd want to explore that further to see where it could lead.

You may have noticed something else about those examples. They're clear enough to follow even though you never saw the opening. More on the importance of clarity later.

One last thing. None of those blurb examples tries to tell the book's story. They're *snippets* of story. They're thin *slices* of the character's situation. They're chosen because they're story elements that show genre and build intrigue at the same time. The lesson is not to say too much. Instead, pick that snippet carefully. Pick individual elements that are representative of the larger story. Don't try to create a synopsis of the plot.

7. Why Nets are Better than Hooks

Commercial fishermen rely on fishing for a living. They don't sit in a boat and dangle a line with a single hook. Instead, they use nets. Big nets.

Doing so, they catch more fish.

Just like professional fishermen, a pro blurb writer disdains the use of a single hook.

You were probably familiar with the idea of opening a blurb with a hook before you started this book. I'll guess as well that you knew it was a good idea to finish with a cliffhanger ending, or open loop now that we're all getting fluent in the language of copywriting.

But where else should we put hooks? Why in those places? And does it matter if they're all the same type of hook?

Natural stopping points

Any text, whether a first chapter of a book, an ad, a webpage or newspaper article, has a series of natural stopping points. These stopping points aren't random. There are triggers for them, and people reevaluate their intentions when they reach them.

By way of example, the end of the first sentence of a book is a natural stopping point. So too the end of the first paragraph. And the second paragraph. Then, more likely, the end of the page. Then the end of the chapter. In web design, above the fold is a natural stopping point. So too a CTA.

None of this is to say that a prospect won't stop reading halfway through a sentence. It's about the concentration of numbers. More people will stop at certain points that at others.

Copywriters know this, and they have an action plan. Wherever there's a stopping point, they embed a hook designed to keep interest high and drive prospects forward. They never, ever, rely on just the opening hook alone. They plant hook after hook through the text, and especially at the natural stopping points. Like a commercial fisherman, they use a net rather than a single hook.

Where are the natural stopping points of a blurb? The end of the tagline or opening sentence is the first. This is quickly followed by the "Read more" CTA. Then the end of every single paragraph. The stopping points are here because it's at these places that a person has finished one chunk of text, and decides whether or not to bother with the next.

These are the places where you want to ensure you have hooks. It's not possible to make every hook perfect, so in terms of priorities the opening is the most important. This gives you momentum, somewhat like pushing a car. It's pretty hard going at first, but once you get on a roll things are easier. You can't stop though because the car will stop if you do. But it does require less effort to keep it rolling than it does to start it moving in the first place.

I should note, the natural stopping points are places where you really must try to insert a hook, but that doesn't mean you can't insert them elsewhere as well.

The beginning of any paragraph is the next best place to the end to insert a hook. This is called frontloading. It's the same principle as frontloading a hook into the opening of the blurb, just on a smaller scale. And, of course, you can slip a hook into the middle of a paragraph as well.

In short, make sure you use a net rather than a lone hook. Don't let an opportunity pass you by to insert a hook anywhere you can, but pay special attention to the natural stopping points. This will funnel the maximum number of prospects through from the first word of the blurb to the last. Statistically, this will net you more sales. People are much, much less likely to buy if they haven't read all the blurb.

By way of example, let's go back to the third paragraph from the blurb for H.M. Ward's *The Arrangement Vol 1*, quoted earlier. This time, I'll inset comments within it in italics.

FML is becoming Avery's motto. *There are two hooks here. The first is a visual one. Remember that we talked about drawing the eye with bold, italics or eye-catching symbols in chapter two? That was for the beginning of a tagline, but the principle is the same here. FML stands out and draws the eye. The second hook is that she has such a motto at all. What's wrong with her life that she thinks that way?* Just when she thinks things couldn't get any worse, they do. *Another hook.* When her car stalls out at a busy intersection and she gets out to check under the hood, a guy steals her car. Armed with a dress and a pair of chucks, Avery runs after the thief. *Another hook. Is she going to catch him? If she does, what's she going to do?* When a hot stranger offers to help, she can't say no. That's how Avery meets Sean Ferro, the totally sexy, totally damaged guy with more secrets than she has time for. *The previous hooks were lightweight. This, at the end of the paragraph, is the heavyweight champion.*

It's worth noting that only a copywriter would see some of these hooks. Especially the FML one. It's not even necessary that the blurb writer planned it that way. Often these things come out instinctively. If H.M. Ward writes her own blurbs, I doubt that she consciously used it with that purpose in mind. But conscious, or inserted only because it "looked right and felt good" comes to the same thing in the end.

Yet the more you analyze blurbs, as we do throughout this book, the more you acquire a conscious skillset and a repertoire of useful tools. Every time you see a blurb you like, or a blurb on the bestseller lists, try to deconstruct it. You'll be amazed at how soon patterns of copywriting techniques begin to emerge, and how your own blurb writing will prosper in response.

Demographic hooks

Not all hooks are created equal.

Different types of hook appeal to different people. To use an analogy, in education, some people are visually orientated, others auditorily and some are hands-on learners. Teachers know this, and they try to present the same material in different manners to ensure each learning preference is catered for.

Copywriters cater for their audience too. Open loops are brilliant, but not everyone has the same sense of curiosity. Every blurb should have multiple open loops, but they should have other types of hook as well to draw in the widest range of prospects. And even open loops themselves come in different shades.

Curiosity drives open loops. But the open loop could be plot based, as in *what* will happen next? Or it could be emotionally based, as in *how* is the hero going to be psychologically or emotionally impacted?

By way of example, here are two open loops. The first is plot based, and the second emotion based.

Frodo must throw the One Ring into the Cracks of Doom. If he fails, the world will fall to ash and ruin. But the Black Riders track him, and they never rest.

Frodo must throw the One Ring into the Cracks of Doom. But undertaking the quest will change him forever. Does he have the courage to try, to say goodbye to the Shire forever?

These are quite similar, but at the same time profoundly different. Those who like character-driven stories will be more intrigued by the second.

It goes without saying (but I'll say it anyway) that the types of hook you use should reflect the genre. An action thriller needs plot hooks. A romance needs emotion hooks. But no reader is exclusively one thing or the other. Use a variety of hooks to draw different people in. And even with the one person, a variety of hooks tugs at them on different levels and intensifies the impact.

There's yet another consideration. A good copywriter knows their audience. That's the golden rule. So, where possible, take the audience into account. Put in triggers that they identify with.

Is your target audience predominantly male or female? Younger? Older? Do they have special interests? For instance, readers of military sci-fi are likely to have a good knowledge of science and military tactics. Ensure you have references to this in the blurb. It needn't be in an open loop. Just slip in a few references here and there to show the story contains the things they like. This is the fact or statement type hook.

The possibilities here are endless. It all depends on what you write, and who the audience is for that type of story. Just be sure to place references in the blurb that they'll understand. It foreshadows the reading experience, and that's a special type of hook all to itself. More on that in a later chapter.

Incidentally, this is one of the reasons editors often don't make good blurb writers. Unless, of course, they're interested in the genre themselves.

Editors omit needless words. That's what they're trained to do. They'll cut out these references, because, to them, they're needless. But they're *not* needless to your target audience. Your target audience will lap them up because they signal the story is of the type they like to read.

8. Interest Ignites Desire

Everything we have gone over so far is building to a purpose. Awareness and attention drive prospects deeper into the blurb. This is where you're doing everything you can to build interest, to take the spark that was there in the beginning and fan it to life.

Now comes the last part of the blurb. You've been stoking interest the way the fire of an old steam train was tended in order to heat water and build pressure to power the engine. If all goes well, you'll reach that magical moment when interest becomes desire.

This *could* happen at the beginning of the blurb, but it's more likely as it progresses. It's most likely in the last paragraph because this is where you throw gas on the flames.

There are several ways to do this. The "gas" is made up of raising the stakes, a twist and a cliffhanger ending. These combine in the last paragraph to set desire alight.

Raising the stakes

Raising the stakes is a standard element of novel writing. It's used to liven things up and intensify the story.

The longer the story, the more this is needed. Otherwise, things become dull and predictable.

But that same livening up is also desirable in a blurb. A sense of rising action and intensified emotions just at the end is a hallmark of the best of them. It brings with it a sense of change and of excitement and of expanding possibilities.

This effect is good in fiction. It's just as good in copywriting. The key to it all is emotion. Raising the stakes puts the hero in greater jeopardy. It intensifies the importance of what they're doing. It allows a blurb of at most two hundred words to reflect some of the three-dimensionality of an entire novel.

In short, it introduces some new element that plants yet another open loop. It's an injection of adrenaline designed to make the heart pump faster. Its purpose is to shift the prospect to a higher state. All the hooks that have gone before draw together on a rising emotional tide. They pull a bit harder, and they help interest transform into desire.

Raising the stakes can be achieved in many ways. Introducing new information that sets a countdown or ticking clock is great. Or a love interest. Or a family member of the hero unexpectedly drawn into jeopardy. It can be lots of things. You get the drift. Pick something suitable for your story and the genre.

The twist

This is similar to raising the stakes. In fact, raising the stakes is inevitably some kind of twist. But in certain genres, for instance thrillers, the twist should be super powerful. It's much more than a twist, but some kind of intense surprise. It becomes its own thing, and it foreshadows that the story itself is full of twists, turns and surprises. This is what readers of the genre are looking for. If the blurb gives them what they want, they'll anticipate the story will too.

So, just like raising the stakes, the twist is attempting to drive the prospect to a higher emotional state, to transform interest into desire.

You can call this a tease if you like. Or an open loop. Certainly, like any good hook, it should be as multilayered as you can make it.

The ending of the blurb is just as important as the opening. At the opening, the prospect decides if they'll bother to keep reading. At the end, they decide what to do next.

This is why it *must* be an open loop. In many situations, a fact or statement type hook serves better as a tagline. This is because interest in a particular subject drives people forward into the blurb. But once they reach the end, you have to leave them with a sense of wanting more. They've become invested now, which they could never be at the start of the blurb.

They like the main character. They identify with the main character. They're convinced the story is of a type they like to read, and that the cover and title didn't mislead them. And investment is the catalyst for desire. This is what you're striving for through the interest phase: to get them invested enough to feel an enormous desire to discover what happens to this character that they've come to *like*.

A cliffhanger ending does this. It's like a text from a person that you're keen on saying, "Meet me for lunch. We need to talk." You don't know what's going on, but you just *have* to find out.

Here's an example. I quote it in full so you can see how the last paragraph builds on everything that's gone before, and guides things to a crescendo. It's the blurb to the kindle edition of Wilbur Smith's *Desert God*.

On the shores of the Nile, the fate of a kingdom rests in one hero's hands…

When the ancient kingdom of Egypt comes under threat, the Pharaoh turns to Taita – freed slave, poet, philosopher and his most trusted advisor – to finally defeat their historic enemy, the Hyksos.

Taita has a cunning plan that will not only deliver a crushing blow to the Hyksos, but will also form a coveted alliance with Crete. In charge of the Pharaoh's sisters, Tehuti and Bekatha as well as a mighty army, Taita embarks on a perilous journey up the Nile, through Arabia to the magical city of Babylon, and across the seas.

But beyond battle and betrayal, there is another danger – the spirited young princesses' attraction to two of the warriors leading the fight could not only ruin Taita's plan but threaten the future of Egypt itself.

This is a blurb that certainly builds. It starts off with a good tagline, fleshes out the main character and a few slices of plot, and then it ratchets up the stakes (already high) in the last paragraph. A new plot thread is introduced, which you could call a twist because it's flipping the blurb somewhat from plot based to character based, but to me it's mostly about making Taita's task harder and the threat to Egypt greater. Thus, it's raising the stakes even higher.

There are a few other things going on. It's a male-centric blurb, that's for sure. Defendable because this is historical fiction, but despite the blurb Wilbur Smith writes some of the strongest female characters I've ever read. Still, I think this is a blurb fault (as is not bolding the tagline and ending the last paragraph with an ellipsis) but all blurbs have faults. No copy is ever prefect.

It's also a good example of resisting the urge to explain things – in other words – avoiding synopsis mode. The word betrayal is thrown in with no background and no context. An editor would likely want to remove it for these reasons, but a copywriter appreciates that it foreshadows to the prospect how much bigger the book is compared to the blurb, and that so much more is happening, and the only way to find anything else out is to buy the book…

Something quite similar is going on with Crete. It weaves into the blurb and then weaves out. And really it could be removed with no consequences.

Except it can't.

Just like the word betrayal, the Crete reference foreshadows that a whole lot more is going on in the story. Actually, it's suggestive of a plot that contains a good dose of political intrigue. Again, editors would be inclined to remove it, but a copywriter knows it's pressing the right buttons for that audience, and is a key trope for many sub-genres of historical fiction.

Remember that we talked about emotional hooks and plot hooks above? Another way to look at "betrayal" and "Crete" is as an emotional and an action hook respectively.

See why I keep talking about layers? That's how great blurbs work. They fit so much into so few words because many of those words are operating at different levels, and for different target audiences, simultaneously.

Best of all, that last paragraph ends with a great cliffhanger. What's going to happen to Egypt? What's going to happen to Taita?

Because earlier parts of the blurb nudge us indirectly to like Taita (who wouldn't like a crafty character who has somehow risen from a slave to become a poet, philosopher and trusted advisor to a Pharaoh?) the cliffhanger at the end is intensified.

This is the perfect way to end a blurb. If this is your kind of story, awareness has evolved into interest, and interest into desire. You *want* to read the book. Hopefully, you even *need* to read the book.

But there's one last part of the sales funnel to go yet. The action part. Is the prospect going to drop everything and buy, or is there still some evaluation left to go?

That's the subject of the next chapter. But one last point here. The cliffhanger is the perfect way to end a blurb. But there may be times when you add an information line afterwards. Only do this if you must, and keep it as short as possible.

An information line might be something like mentioning the book is a boxed set of a completed series. If that's the case, it has to be mentioned somewhere. It's a selling point. It can't interrupt the blurb itself, so that leaves the opening or the end. If you have a good tagline, that means it goes to the end. But keep it short, otherwise it dilutes the power of the cliffhanger hook.

There you have it. That's the best way to end a blurb. Raise the stakes and use a cliffhanger. Put in a twist too, if you can manage it.

9. The Invisible Hand

The end of the blurb is a crossroads. The prospect has choices about what to do next, and they know it. They'll have long since established a behavior pattern, and trying to interfere with that is like asking a fidgety person to stop fidgeting.

Buying is certainly one of their options, but Amazon's web design shows it's an option few people take just at that point. If they did, Amazon would have a buy CTA right there in that spot. And they don't.

Deducing customer behavior from web design is one way to go. But we have more proof of customer behavior in this case. Reviews are important to many, many people, as a Google search for "importance of online reviews" will show.

People don't buy something, and then read the reviews afterward. Reading the reviews forms part of many people's evaluation process.

We also know that the preview forms a large part of the evaluation phase. And given that Amazon *do* place a buy CTA at its end, I'd suggest that Amazon's data shows that's where the majority of "buy" clicks occur. That's just a deduction though, and it can't be relied on.

One way or another, the end of the blurb is still a crossroads where the prospect has multiple valid options that could eventually lead to a sale. We just don't know which path is their established buying pattern.

In short, it's a copywriter's nightmare.

What's needed is a CTA to the reviews, at least for the prospects who look at reviews. But we also need a CTA to the preview for the prospects who use *that* to evaluate.

But it's a principle of copywriting that multiple CTAs in the one place don't work. Doing that is like having two teachers giving a kid in school conflicting orders at the same time.

It's in situations like this that a marketer has to dig deeper. They need to go beyond the superficial aspects of copywriting. They have to consider the true psychological state of the prospect. And from that they can draw on their deeper-level knowhow to nudge the person further down the sales funnel.

When you look at the crossroads problem clearly, the answer becomes clear. The prospect will have already formed a view as to whether or not they like what they've seen, but they have more evaluating to do before their final decision.

Looking at reviews is more of a confirmation thing. They like what they see, and they want to *reassure* themselves that their opinion is shared. They're seeking social proof, and the reviews will hopefully offer that.

The reviews also serve to advise if the book is full of typos or has some sort of major problem. Perhaps the prospect hates cliffhanger endings, or swearing, or whatever their personal "do not buy" triggers are. This is fair enough. That's what reviews are for.

The same applies for previews. The prospect likes the blurb, but it's sensible to actually read the beginning pages of the book to see if it resonates.

Most prospects will probably do both, so we need one CTA that nudges people in their preferred direction, whichever it is.

Impossible.

And yet, it isn't.

The purpose of a CTA is usually twofold. It's designed to nudge people in a certain direction, and to give them clarity about how to actually act once their decision is made.

This last part is the key. It's critical in some CTAs. This is why we have "Click to download", or "Start here". That type of CTA provides a nudge, but it also lets the prospect know *how* to do what's required. It saves the prospect looking all over the place for instructions on how to do what they want.

The nudge part of a CTA is a feature of every CTA. The giving clarity part on how to do something is optional. In the case of Amazon shoppers, they know exactly how to scroll down to the reviews or reach the preview. The explanation isn't required.

This solves our problem. We want to nudge them forward, but we don't need to give them instructions on how to do it.

Enter the covert CTA (as opposed to the overt CTA). Much of marketing is influenced by subconscious things, and subliminal marketing is a whole field to itself. I suggest you Google this because it's fascinating. Or just take a look at the Amazon logo for confirmation that multibillion-dollar corporations take this stuff seriously. See how the curved arrow under their name forms a smiley face, subconsciously suggesting that shopping with them is a positive experience?

But most importantly for us right now, the key concept is that the best marketing is invisible. It operates below the radar. The worst marketing is obvious. Prospects feel manipulated, and they resent it. Who blames them?

In behavioral psychology, the term for this is "reactance". Reactance has the effect of strengthening people's motivation to do the *opposite* of what they're being asked to do. This is poor marketing indeed.

A "buy now" CTA is commonplace in many, many situations. In those places, it's so common that people don't even notice it.

But it's not common at the end of a blurb. It stands out like a guy leaping from a plane without a parachute, and is therefore a high risk of triggering reactance.

In the case of a blurb, not only does a covert CTA work better, but there's a brilliant one that drives people forward through the rest of the sales funnel, and it doesn't matter if the prospect wants to look at reviews, read a preview … or phone a friend.

It's called a cliffhanger. We discussed it before. A good one leaves the prospect *needing* to find out more. Its power comes from the open hooks of the blurb, all firing up to a crescendo at the end, and from liking the main character. It's stronger by far than any "buy now" or "grab your copy today" CTA will *ever* be. And it's nondiscriminatory. It'll drive people to reviews, if that's where they want to go. Or the preview.

The cliffhanger is like an invisible hand that leads someone forward along the sales funnel. It doesn't care which route they take. It just guides them where they want to go, offering steady support all the way to make sure they get there.

If you've learned anything here, it's this. Good marketing is covert rather than overt. The best marketing is *invisible*.

Alternatively, you may have learned this. KISS. Keep it simple, stupid.

Book blurbs have existed for over a hundred years. They work well just as they are, and prospects prefer what they're familiar with. Buying is about trust. Blurbs don't need remodeling with a misplaced buy CTA any more than the wheel needs remodeling into a square.

10. The True Power of Emotion

This is something I learned in my government job trying to convince people to comply with their tax requirements. If the taxpayer believed they already were in compliance with the legislation, then often no amount of evidence, logic, facts, figures, ramifications, case law, notification of potential penalties or legal advice would change their mind.

Belief is *stronger* than facts. In neuroscience, this is called priors. Trying to change someone's mind is near impossible. Many of these people, despite every opportunity to do what was required, ultimately paid extra tax and penalties on top of the tax after legal action was taken to force them to comply.

It wasn't a nice situation. I hated it. They hated it more.

But what did I learn from it? I looked deeper into the science of persuading people, and I discovered that one of the most powerful methods to do so was to invoke emotion.

The part of the brain that deals with emotion (the amygdala) is older than the parts that deal with rational thought. In many ways, this part is more powerful and exerts a profound (if hidden) influence on our decisions. And this is a potent concept used by copywriters.

I incorporated this new approach into our compliance program, and voluntary compliance increased and legal action decreased. It was a win for everybody because despite common opinion, the government only takes someone to court as a very last resort.

You may find it hard to believe that people ignored all the information at hand that should have proven to them that they were in trouble and convinced them to act. I did too.

But it happened again and again. Until we modified our approach. I turned things on their head, and stopped trying to convince them of anything. This was only causing reactance. It wasn't easy because government departments tend to keep on doing what they've always done. The *belief* of the powers that be (priors) was that what they were doing, what they had always done, was the best way.

This is why in this book I try to convince you of nothing. I give you some information, and then I ask you to research it for yourselves. I say, again and again, not to take my word for anything, nor anyone else's. You can do that and form your own opinion.

And guess what? You have an emotional investment in your own opinion. Inner belief and emotion are stronger than intellectual arguments.

How does any of this help blurb writing? It's at the *core* of blurb writing. This is why I've been at pains to offer up the combined tactics of ensuring the prospect likes your main character, identifies with them and feels some sort of emotion about them or their situation.

This is incredibly powerful, and invoking sympathy is the most powerful tactic of all and the easiest to achieve in the extremely short window of opportunity that a blurb allows.

Mirror neurons are how this is done. Let me repeat that. Mirror neurons. Better still, go Google them.

Or, if you're still here, this next bit will fire yours up. Nothing like a live experiment to help you remember something. It's even better than repetition.

Imagine you're watching one of those medical reality TV shows. The patient is an old man, and he's wheeled on a stretcher into the emergency department. Tears stream down his left cheek. The left side of his face is swollen. His hands are balled into fists because of pain. The doctor asks what happened, and the man manages to croak out an answer. *A wasp stung me right on the eye...*

Ouch! Did that make you cringe? That's mirror neurons at work. Our brain is hardwired so that certain neurons fire when we do something, and those same neurons fire when we *observe* someone else perform the same action.

Scientists speculate that this is a learning mechanism because copying is fundamental to the way humans grow and develop.

But it goes deeper. Mirror neurons are believed to be involved with empathy. Experiments show that certain areas of the brain are active when they experience an emotion *and* when they see another person experience an emotion.

This is what you want in your blurb. Empathy. Emotion sells better than logic. Give your prospect reasons to empathize with your main character, and they'll become invested in the future of that character. Induce sympathy, and you've magnified the effect. Sympathy is incredibly powerful.

This is a pretty high-level technique. Marketers have long used it, but it's nice to know the scientific explanation for *why* it works.

Copywriters have another trick for this too. Certain words are more likely to be felt on an emotional level than others. I'm not aware of any science behind this, but it's a common practice and you may feel the truth of it when I give you some examples. Or you may not. See what you think, anyway.

Which of these words strikes the more acute emotional cord?

Love / affection
Hate / animosity
Sad / dismal
Fear / terror
Anger / acrimony

The words on the left are all native English words, coming down to us today through a long history of Germanic etymology stretching into unrecorded antiquity. Their synonyms on the right are a much more recent layer of vocabulary derived from Latin and French.

All I can say is that if you propose marriage to someone, I'd recommend saying you love them and not that you have affection for them.

For whatever reason, the native words resonate better on an emotional level. This is not to say that native words are better than imported ones. Just that they're different. I suggest using the native ones when you want to hit home with an emotion, but the imported ones often provide shades of meaning and gravitas. For instance, I used the imported words "unrecorded antiquity" just before. Something like "unwritten oldness" just doesn't have the same ring to it.

I've scrunched a few concepts together in this chapter. I did this because they all relate strongly to each other. But they *are* separate concepts, and I suggest you look into them individually if time and desire permit. The first two are critical to understand if you wish to hone your copywriting skills. The third, while useful, is not essential.

So, to summarize a complex chapter, these are the three take-home points.

Firstly, pre-existing belief is stronger than facts. You'll rarely convince anyone of anything by trying to talk them into it, even if it's logical. Making the attempt is bad marketing. Be wary of a CTA in the wrong place. Be wary of telling someone *why* they should buy your book. Reactance is likely.

Secondly, good marketing leaves people freedom of choice and options. Instead of trying to convince them of something, appeal to them on an emotional level. This is far more powerful in the long run. Trigger a liking for your character in the blurb, and put them in an emotional situation. The prospect's mirror neurons will fire, and they'll have greater investment in the story. Intensify this with sympathy, and you're backing a winner.

Thirdly, try to use emotive words, which will often be native English words, to keep building the prospect's emotional connection.

Are these things brilliant marketing tactics? Are they just common sense? Or are they simply good writing habits?

You decide.

11. Clarity

This will be a short chapter.

Clarity is not a marketing tactic. But without it, your marketing tactics, however cutting-edge they are, however fancy, however subtle, will be in vain.

Imagine this. A builder constructs a mansion. On the top story is a special room with a view of the surrounding countryside. In the distance, snow-capped mountains march. Their lower slopes are swathed by the dark green of pine forests. In the foreground rests a silver lake, the essence of tranquility.

That's quite a view. Yes?

Now imagine the builder placed frosted glass in the windows. All that view is lost because of a structural fault…

In a blurb, clear writing enables the prospect to see, at a glance, all the promise of the story. This is what you want.

Poor writing obstructs their view.

I should say poor *copywriting* obstructs their view.

Copywriting is a specialist skill. It takes years, even decades, of working at the craft to master it. You don't obtain that level of skill reading a few books on the subject.

But few of you reading this book want to be professional copywriters. You just want to learn how to write a great blurb. Yes?

The good news is this is relatively easy. You don't need all the tools of the professional copywriter. You just need to know the handful that apply to blurbs.

But this much is still true. No matter that a blurb is a tiny slice of the copywriting pie, it's still copywriting. The first step to getting good at it is to recognize that it is *not* normal writing. Copywriting will employ methods and styles that may be at odds with what your editor says.

Keep that in mind. And remember that copywriting will not use *The Chicago Manual of Style*, or some other style guide. The purpose of copywriting is to sell. The purpose of style guides has nothing whatsoever to do with that. Nothing.

But good copywriting and good writing intersect in many places. The catchphrase of "omit needless words" is one.

Omit needless words. This is an important part of clarity. The catchphrase comes from that famous style guide, *The Elements of Style*.

At the risk of missing the mark on brevity, which is another hallmark of clarity, I'll say this for no other reason than it's interesting. One of the authors of *The Elements of Style* was E.B. White. Mr. White was many things. Journalist. Editor. Fiction writer. But he was also a professional *copywriter*. He knew what he was about, and clarity and brevity are features of his style guide. They're two areas where good copywriting and good writing intersect.

Other areas – not so much. Here are a few subheadings and discussions. Some of these things your editor will like. Others, maybe not. Remember to evaluate based on copywriting intentions and not standard writing advice.

Name soup

This is a common issue, and likely enough you'll have heard the term before.

This is the thing to remember. You know your story and your characters. You know their names and their motivations and what their favorite breakfast is. The prospect knows *nothing*. Keep it simple for them, or else it's like they've gone to a party and been introduced to ten people in a matter of seconds. It's too much and too confusing. Everything will be jumbled.

Instead, I suggest you use only the names of characters (and places) that you must. If the name isn't there to gain attention, build interest, desire, simplify some aspect of plot or for some other vital reason, leave it out. This includes the second name of the protagonist. If dropping it in isn't serving some justifiable purpose, kick it out again.

All this applies doubly if your names are unusual in some way, which is often the case in fantasy and science fiction.

Plot soup

This is as common a problem as name soup, but I suspect I've coined the description for it here. Instead of choosing a slice of plot to highlight in the blurb, or a few slices, the blurb writer tries to represent the whole cake by taking tiny slivers from all around it.

Let's follow through with that example. You can tell someone that you had a Black Forest cake for dessert. Or you can tell them that you had a cake of German origin, made with eggs, sugar, flour, cocoa powder, butter, vanilla extract, kirsch and cream. And it was topped with cherries.

The second option is more comprehensive, but no more effective than the first. In fact, listing the ingredients is downright boring.

People know what a black forest cake is. Tell them that, or show them a picture on your phone, and they'll recognize it at a glance.

Back to blurbs. Just pick a few elements of the plot and tease them out. Use ones that show genre, and that allow you to layer emotion and hooks over the top of them. That's all you need.

Less is more.

A triad of shortness

Short words. Short sentences. Short paragraphs. These three things are the besties of copywriting. They make it easy to read and to understand. This is what you want.

Elongated vocabulary expressed in syntactically complex style over a protracted length is disharmonious to the surveying gaze and causes that which is simple to be perceived as a matter of excruciating reconditeness.

This is not what you want.

But, and there's always a but, take your target audience into account. If you're writing a blurb for highbrow literary fiction, they may not respond to a smooth and simple blurb style. They'll want to see that you're a master of the long sentence and inscrutable complexity.

Give them what they want.

Whitespace

Whitespace aids readability. It's that simple. Almost. It does one more thing too, which takes us back to the phenomenon of the halo effect.

Whitespace gives the impression of simplicity.

Before a prospect begins to read a blurb, the overall image of what the text looks like makes an impression on them. I don't mean the words here, or how it reads. I mean that the text is *literally* seen as a single image first, something like a picture.

That split-second initial picture is all that it takes for a reader to form an opinion. A wall of text will give the appearance of something difficult to read. Whitespace will give the impression of something easy to read, and *well written*.

The second impression will lead to more people actually reading the blurb, and a more favorable opinion of it. This initial favorable opinion carries through as they read. This is what the halo effect does. It flavors opinion like the odor of garlic in the fridge taints everything in there with it.

Only the halo effect does it in a good way.

Readability score

Most writing and editing software have readability scores built into them. This is useful. Microsoft Word uses the Flesch-Kincaid test, and what you're looking for with that is a score of about 80 to 90. If you're coming in somewhere in the 70s, I suggest having a close look at things to see if you can make your blurb more readable.

If you're coming in below 60, we need to have a talk.

Seriously. Remember that this is copywriting and not normal writing. The better the readability of the blurb, the better it will move prospects through the sales funnel. The prospect has no investment in you or your book. None at all, unless they're already fans. They're only giving you a few seconds of their busy lives. Make it easy for them.

Readability is a fine balance though. What you're aiming for is something super-readable, and yet that at the same time that looks like normal prose.

Anyone can…

…Write paragraphs like…

This, and score well.

That approach is sometimes recommended for blurbs. But it's not good copywriting. It's dumbing down. It draws attention to itself, especially in an ecosystem made up of readers like Amazon, and it attracts the risk of being seen to be manipulative.

Being seen to be manipulative is one of the biggest sales killers of all time. It fires up reactance. Treat your prospects with respect. Make it easy for them, but don't insult their intelligence.

Em dashes, colons and semi colons

Any editors reading this are going to hate me. They love punctuation. And for good reason. Good punctuation aids clarity.

But I don't use these forms of punctuation in copywriting.

I touched on the reason earlier. When a prospect first opens a page, paper or electronic, that first nanosecond of vision is like a picture of the whole. Block paragraph, and dashes and dots and squiggles, will make that picture seem cluttered. It's not the impression you want to give.

A moment later the prospect's gaze is drawn to the top left, at least if they're European. That's where Westerners are accustomed to text starting.

But a similar thing happens when they begin to read. The gaze takes in a little more than one word at a time. An impression of the rest of the paragraph is formed, another picture if you will, but this one is smaller. Again, lines, dots and squiggles will make it look cluttered. Even academic.

All this is the opposite of what a copywriter wants. A copywriter hopes for the text to be invisible (apart from exceptions such as taglines) and for the words to jump out from the page and slide deftly into the prospect's mind.

I said academic before, and with good reason. These types of punctuation marks not only look cluttered, but they're the hallmark of complex academic or legalese jargon.

Copywriters avoid them like the plague, just the same as they avoid beating a dead horse with stale clichés...

The em dash is the worst offender—joining two words together and making them appear strange and complex.

Commas are another matter because they're near invisible and allow the sentence to flow smoothly.

The en dash

I'm not prejudiced against en dashes. Unlike their show-pony bigger brother, the em dash, who tries to steal the limelight and attract attention to itself, the en dash doesn't connect to the words on either side, and it's smaller.

The en dash isn't near-invisible like a comma, but it has one great advantage – it makes prose look conversational. A neat trick – often used by copywriters to good effect.

Action and reaction / cause and effect

A lack of logical sequencing contributes to a lack of clarity. Look at these examples.

Frodo ran, and a Black Rider reared up behind him.

A Black Rider reared up behind Frodo, and he ran.

The first puts the reaction ahead of the cause. This causes the reader a momentary stumble. The second puts the cause first and the reaction second, in logical sequence. It's clearer.

Not much of a difference, to be sure. But it can add up if it happens several times. More importantly, achieving clarity is the result of using a whole bunch of good-writing tactics at the same time.

There are exceptions to the action and reaction logic. It's not a rule. Nothing I say is ever a rule. There's only one rule in copywriting – and that's to do what works.

Sentence fragments

Again, editors and copywriters are at odds here. Editors tend to hate sentence fragments, and copywriters love them.

Sentence fragments are conversational. Because of their pithy brevity, they give words more power. They're great for expressing attitude, which we'll come to in the chapter on voice. They provide emphasis. They let you say more with less, saving you space and contributing to clarity. *Awesome!*

I just love sentence fragments. Most copywriters use them frequently. This is another area of research worth a bit of Google time.

The ellipsis

This doesn't really have much to do with clarity. I include it in this chapter because, like sentence fragments, it says more with less – and saying more with less does contribute something to clarity.

The ellipsis has a special place in the copywriting hall of fame. It's the *ultimate* example of less is more. Those mere dots represent a world of meaning. They convey that so much more is going on than has been said, and they intensify a sense of mystery wherever they appear.

An ellipsis is a type of hook all to itself. It foreshadows that something is going to happen, but gives away none of the details. If you had to designate a symbol that represented hooks in the way that the yin and yang symbol represents an entire philosophy of life, you would choose an ellipsis.

But a word of warning. Like all things in marketing, less is more. Be wary of overusing it. I would say no more than twice in a blurb.

And when you do use it, use it wisely. As I've tried to show all the way through this book, the art of copywriting comes in layers. Attach an ellipsis to a genuine hook. They'll work together synergistically to produce the best result. An ellipsis by itself will try its best, but that's like asking a surgeon to operate in your living room. Give her a hospital theater and access to medical equipment, and the results will be better.

Speaking of results, the next chapter will reveal the secret of taking a blurb to the next level…

12. The Secret Sauce

The secret sauce is voice.

Few blurbs have it. Those that do, sing. Voice is that special something that lifts a blurb from the anonymity of sounding like a million others, and it gives it character, mood or flare.

Voice is the last layer to go onto the blurb. When you are done with hooks, plot, interest, desire and weaving emotions through your copy, you're seeking to tease out its voice and enrich it.

What *is* voice?

There are some much better qualified to answer that question than I am. But I have an opinion on the subject, and I'll share it. You figured I would, yes?

Voice in blurbs comes in different forms. These are the most common.

A conversational style

Romance and urban fantasy are the true home for this, though you'll see it in other places too. It's light and sharp and witty. It's like the blurb is your best friend, whispering away in your ear. It's like someone you've known all your life.

What it's not like is a grandfatherly editor style blurb, all stiff and formal, wearing a cardigan and smelling vaguely of camphor and emotional distance because you only visit every third Christmas.

The conversational style is usually in first person, but not always. It'll use asides and en dashes. It'll be in your face, but in a good way. And if you let it, it'll charm your socks off and lure you into the book quicker than you can say antidisestablishmentarianism.

High style

This is the calling card of some types of epic fantasy. But I've seen it in science fiction too.

It's the opposite of conversational. It's not distant like the grandfatherly editor. It's like the voice of your forefathers of remote antiquity calling to you across a dark span of years. It's sparse and remote. It's poetic too. The magic of it is like an echo of far off times, and for those who yearn to hear such a thing, no music is sweeter.

A sense of humor

This one is self-explanatory. It can be witty like urban fantasy blurbs, or it can be dark. It can be snarky. Or sarcastic. Or it can be dry and understated. Whatever it is, it's hard to pull off because humor is subjective.

Obviously, you can break voice down beyond these three categories. It has no limit, because ultimately it derives from the worldview and character of the writer. And how much of that they're willing to reveal to the world. This is why voice is hard to achieve. It requires baring the soul.

The voice of the blurb should reflect the book, at least to some extent. There are more exceptions to this than you might think, which I'll tackle shortly.

But first, an example. This is from *A Thirst for Vengeance,* by Edward M. Knight. It's epic fantasy.

My name is Dagan. There are few alive who have more blood on their hands than I.

I have lived a life of degeneracy. I have studied the teachings of the dark mage Helosis and walked the path of the dead. I have been to the shadowrealm and emerged with my soul intact. I have challenged the Black Brotherhood and ridden with the Knights of Valamor as brother-in-arms. I have spoken to Xune.

I've killed indiscriminately—for money, for fame. For vengeance.

When I was young, I fell in love with a princess and was punished by her death. I have scampered, begged, and thieved. I have been homeless. I have ruled the greatest city ever built.

I began a succession war. I alone know who lifted the Seals of Regor—and how. I was there when magic was restored to this world. If I'd been born in a different age, I would have been the greatest sorcerer known to man.

My name is Dagan. This is my tale.

That's a lot of blurb. It has a good tagline, and to me at least, it has great voice. So strong is this voice that it masks some grave blurb errors.

The blurb is all backstory. It has no conflict, and no story goal. You know at the outset, that despite the things that have happened, Dagan is alive to tell you his story.

But despite those shortcomings, it was a bigtime bestseller. Just goes to prove that there's no such thing as blurb rules.

It's the voice, I believe, that made that book sell. And the blurb does have a few other things going for it that we've talked about. The tagline is good. It's a nice, juicy open loop. How could you read that, and not want to find out more?

There are elements of sympathy. There are hooks planted in the text as well. But throwing all those strange names around can also read like a shopping list. But the voice carries the prospect through it all, and the next best feature is the tension created by the contrast. It's a blurb of *extreme* contrasts, and that contributes to the voice because it resonates with life experience. Life is like that, and it gives the blurb a three-dimensional consistency. So too the emotion woven throughout it.

That's voice. I could give other examples, but if you want to dig deeper urban fantasy blurbs are probably the best place to study it. Closely followed by romance.

Now, a few technical issues.

By tradition, blurbs are written in present tense. Is there a valid reason for this?

The tense certainly has an impact on voice. Present tense isn't normal in other aspects of fiction. Virtually all fiction is past tense. So present tense in a blurb stands out against that background.

This is a good thing for sales copy. On the other hand, a browser on Amazon checking out books is well used to reading them in present tense. The blurb before was present tense. The blurb after will be present tense. Present tense is the norm here, and therefore invisible.

That gives rise to a thought though. A copywriter wants their copy to stand out. It's more likely to be read through that way. Would a blurb in past tense, or for that matter future tense, stand out? Would it garner more attention?

It's an interesting thought. Really, it needs testing. But it's near impossible (or actually impossible) to test blurbs. More on that later.

Still, it's a tempting proposition. I haven't tried it. I'm not aware that anyone has. Past tense has certainly occurred, but that's by accident when people didn't know the convention is for present tense. Future tense would stand out even more though. It would be quite different. For that reason, it would be a high-risk strategy. For that same reason, I don't recommend it. But if you're a risk taker, and if it fitted well with your voice, then it might be worth a chance to try it out and see how the dice rolled.

Of course, writers know that blurbs should be in present tense. They'd all shake their heads at you thinking you were an idiot. Copywriters though ... they'd prick their ears and study your blurb *very* closely. The truth is though, neither writers nor copywriters are your target audience. What they think is irrelevant. All that counts is what your readers think. More accurately, all that counts is how your readers act.

Back to present tense. Does it have anything going for it apart from convention?

It does. Present tense invokes urgency and immediacy (because it gives a sense the events are happening now, and aren't already done and dusted) that past doesn't quite match. Not in the short parameters of a blurb. Fiction is different. Given a bit of time and space, a writer can lure readers into any modality. Even first person present tense. But blurbs don't have the luxury of time. They have the life expectancy of a mayfly on life support.

This gives rise to another benefit of present tense. It's often used in sales copy because simple present tense tends to take up less space. That was a bigger factor where the practice originally arose – in newspaper headlines and ad copy in papers and magazines where every character counted. It's not *quite* so relevant to blurbs that have much more space available to them.

So, present tense has some advantages. It has a tradition behind it. But if your voice takes you away from that, so be it. Voice and character in a blurb will trump convention any day of the week.

There's another blurb convention. They're supposed to be written in third person, even if the book is in first.

There's no copywriting reason for this. So far as I can tell, there's no reason at all for it. Break the convention at will. Indies in romance and urban fantasy do all the time. For them, the convention has pretty much become first person, and third person is becoming somewhat unusual. All I'd say is that you should know what the convention is in your genre. You won't go wrong following that.

But again, if we dig deeper, first person has an advantage over third. It, like present tense, creates a greater sense of immediacy and also a deeper sense of connection in the short parameters of a blurb. This is a distinct benefit.

Against that, some people just don't read first person books. So it comes down to this, as it always does with copywriting – know your audience.

Here's a little-known fact. Some books written in third person have blurbs written in first. And I doubt it's by accident. Check out *Moth* by Daniel Arenson. Better still, check out the Kindle-edition blurb for *Magician* by Raymond E. Feist.

The bottom line is that you're free to do what suits you and your audience best.

Time to talk about adjectives. Most writing advice tells you to limit adverbs. Sometimes adjectives get caught up in this. You'll have a personal preference one way or the other. But whatever style you prefer for fiction, always keep in mind that copywriting is *not* fiction.

Do you ever see an ad for a resort? I don't. They're always for an *island* resort. Or a *tropical-paradise* resort. Do you ever see an ad for a phone? Or are they *high-tech* phones? Or *compact* phones? Or *lightweight* phones? Is a sale ever a sale? Or is it a *clearance* sale? Or a *massive* sale? Or a *crazy* sale?

Adjectives paint a picture. That picture helps a prospect envision the product as more desirable. This helps turn a prospect into a buyer.

As always, make your own mind up. For myself, I limit adverbs. But I use adjectives wherever a good one turns a noun into a rip-roaring noun.

One last word on voice – one last comment on the difference between editor and copywriter.

Editors work to a style guide. It doesn't matter which one, because the differences between them are subtle. Pretty much every influence on an editor is pushing them in the same direction. Omit needless words. Avoid passive voice. Avoid adverbs. Avoid sentence fragments. Choose vivid nouns. Choose active verbs. Avoid nonstandard English. Avoid qualifiers. Don't start a sentence with a dependent clause. Put statements in a positive form. Don't dangle participles. Avoid ending a sentence with a preposition. Not sure what that last one is good for. But it's supposed to make your writing better.

Well, now for something that copywriters avoid. Editor's voice. All those rules push editors in the same direction. After a while, they each sound just like the other. When one claps their hands, they all do. When one stands on tiptoe and pats their head while rubbing their tummy, they all do.

It's a rare editor who breaks free and finds their writer's voice. Rarer still for one to find a copywriter's voice. Doing either means tossing aside many of the rules they've learned. Remember that neuroscience term of priors? It's at play here.

I'm not having a go at editors. Or writers who follow the same style guides. I'm just pointing out that this is one of the differences between sales copy and other forms of writing.

Editor's voice, all smooth and perfect and correct, is monotonous. Editor's voice is the death of sales. How many times has a prospect read that same style before?

Copywriting tries to break through the monotony. It dodges and turns and twists. It'll reach out of the page and grab the reader by the throat – in a good way. It's never the bad boy at a party. But it's always the rogue with a cheeky grin and an all-too-innocent expression.

Tread your own path, grasshopper.

13. Why Common Blurb Formulas Fail

There are quite a few blurb formulas floating around. You'll probably have seen them. They all make some good points. But they all *fail* as sales copy too.

Why?

First, let's run through a few of them. Then I'll show you the key reason they don't work well.

This seems to be the one in most common use.

> Who is the hero?
> What does he/she want?
> What is the conflict?
> What must the hero do?
> What is at stake?

It covers some good ground, and all its points are valid. These are good things to include in a blurb. Here's another.

> Who is the hero and what's going on in their life?
> What is the Big Problem?
> What are the biggest obstacles the hero has to face?
> What is at stake?

It's a variation of the first, but not the same.

> Setting
> Conflict
> Objective
> Possible solution

Emotional promise

That one introduces a few new elements.

When (insert protagonist's name)
Does (insert something)
Something happens (insert what)
Now with (insert time limit/restrictions)
The protagonist must (insert something brave)
To (insert a great accomplishment)
Or (insert high stakes)

That is really quite different and *very* specific.

Introduce your main character(s)
Set the stage for your primary conflict
Establish the stakes
Show the reader why this book is for them

That one has elements of the others, but differences too.

Situation
Problem
Promise a twist
Emphasize mood of the story

Another one with some common elements but also some new material.

Backstory
Main characters
Main conflict

That one has the advantage of brevity, at least.

Enough of blurb formulas. Those are the main ones, but there are lots of variations.

Do you see the flaw with every one of them?

I'll tell you what I see. They all make good points about the kind of things that should go into a blurb. But *none* of them are structured in a way that acknowledges buyer behavior. This is because none of the formulas are copywriter based.

A copywriter knows the critical importance of attracting eyeballs to the opening. They know that without getting awareness and snaring attention, prospects won't read the rest of the blurb. They know why Amazon doesn't even bother to show the blurb in full. *Most prospects don't read beyond the opening.*

These formulas fail on that ground alone. But it's a fail of monumental proportions.

But what about a blurb ending? Having read the earlier chapters in this book, you know how critical it is to leave the prospect with a cliffhanger ending that will drive them farther through the sales funnel to the reviews or preview.

How do these formulas fare on that score? None of them have anything to say about it. So, the two most important pieces of blurb real estate, the beginning and the end, are void of marketing considerations.

Another way of saying this is that the formulas don't adhere to the scientifically established model of buyer behavior that marketers call the sales funnel. They don't address the awareness and action phase in the funnel at all.

This is no surprise. Writers and editors developed those formulas. Not copywriters.

They do have good points though. They work well enough for the interest phase of the sales funnel.

This leaves us with a simple question. What formula would a marketer use?

As it happens, there are lots of formulas that marketers use. The oldest and the best is called AIDA.

Attention
Interest
Desire
Action

Sound familiar? It should do. It's basically the sales funnel itself. It's a prompt that copywriters use to remind themselves to tune each part of their copy to the buying stages the prospect goes through as they read it.

It's nonrestrictive too. It lets you do things your way, and the way that suits your story and voice. And no matter how weird and wonderful and different your blurb is, if it's taking the prospect through the buying stages it's working.

Don't take my word for it. Google AIDA. See the formula a professional copywriter would use to write a fiction blurb (nonfiction is different). Study up on it. Research it. Look for that formula at play on bestselling book blurbs, posters for movies, ads on TV for dishwashing liquid and pretty much everywhere you turn your gaze. Because professional marketing is *everywhere*.

Make AIDA your own. Understand it intimately. It'll inform every marketing decision you make from writing a blurb to sending a new-release alert to your newsletter list, or getting subscribers on that list in the first place.

I'd even go so far as to say that once you grasp how important AIDA is to an indie author, every aspect of your publishing business will improve and sales will increase. It's the single most important tool at your disposal.

Google it. Study it. Make it your own.

14. How Long should a Blurb be?

It's a simple question. But it has no easy answer. A similar question is asked about stories. How long should they be? The answer often given to that one is as long as it takes to tell the story.

We can do better than that. I *hate* that for an answer. It's meaningless and provides no actionable information. But what do I know? When that question is asked, that's the answer always given.

So, I'll give a specific and actionable answer for blurbs. In copywriting terms, there *is* an answer. A blurb, just like any sales copy, has to take the prospect through the sales funnel. It must attract attention, develop interest and transform that into desire so that the prospect becomes ready to act.

Another copywriting principle is that the more expensive the product, or the higher the psychological barriers that need to be overcome in order to get a sale, the longer the copy needs to be.

Never be misled by people who say copy should be short. Never be misled by people who say copy should be long. Always look at it from the point of view of the prospect, and what they want and are used to seeing in the particular ecosystem in which you're selling.

Let's break it down. The blurb opening needs to attract attention. It needs to show the prospect that it's worth their while to invest a bit more time reading the full blurb. One line is enough for this. But that depends on your opening. Review quotes will take longer. So will a few other things. So, to put a word count on it, I would say anything below about 50 words. If you haven't got the prospect's attention by then, you're in serious trouble.

How long does it take to develop interest and transform it into desire? I place these two concepts together, because it's a work in progress. It's a building of investment. It doesn't happen at the flick of a switch. Interest and desire telescope together.

I would say that if you haven't done this in less than 100 words, then once again you're in trouble. And you're probably trying to summarize the whole story rather than throw a beam of light on just a few slices of the plot.

Action. How long should this phase be? This is where the stakes rise and there's some sort of surprise, twist or new information. This takes longer than the opening. But not as much as interest and desire. So, I'd give it about 75 words.

That makes for a *maximum* total of about 225 words. To counterbalance that, I'd also say that you can't go through the whole AIDA formula (in a book blurb) in less than 75 words. Fewer than that, and you're just not meeting prospect expectations for how long a blurb should be, nor giving them sufficient chance to evaluate it properly. And if you try to shortchange their evaluation time, they won't buy.

This leaves us with a sweet spot of around 150 words. It's also right there in terms of prospect expectations for how long a blurb should be. A blurb that length is neither long nor short.

150 words is the Goldilocks length. If in doubt, aim for pretty close to that. On the other hand, if you write one much shorter or longer, and you think it's a cracker, go with it.

Nothing I say here, or anywhere else, is meant to be a rule. Frankly, I don't believe in rules. The moment you lay one down, you'll find an exception to it. And if there's one exception, there are others.

Develop your skill at writing copy, and then learn to trust your gut instinct for what's working and what isn't. Unless, of course, you can split test. But this isn't easy on Amazon.

15. Can You Test Blurb Performance?

You want the short answer?

Despite what some people say, no you can't. No way. Nope. Ain't gonna work. Hopeless. No chance.

Here's the long answer.

Any such test would have to be on Amazon (and the other retailers if you're wide). It must test actual prospects and test them on the platform through which they buy. If it's not doing this, then you can't rely on the results any more than testing a drug on a mouse and concluding it works for humans. This is why scientists test on humans as well, and frequently the results of animal tests are *not* replicated. People aren't mice. Facebook and the like aren't Amazon.

So, setting up Facebook ads and sending the prospect to one of your webpages where you can split test blurbs is testing *Facebook* users. And you can't know if those Facebook users are representative of your actual target audience on Amazon, or not. In fact, generally they're not. There's plenty of evidence from people running Facebook ads that the results skew toward sales rather than Kindle Unlimited borrows. That's just one known difference. There would be other differences in behavior too.

At any rate, few people use this method. More in vogue is to run one blurb on Amazon for a certain period of time, and then an alternative blurb for the same period. Sales and borrows are then compared. If desired, this process can be repeated.

Well, in my view, this method is even more flawed than the Facebook method.

Sales figures, and borrow volume, fluctuate considerably on Amazon. Here are a few of the reasons.

Sales typically follow a bell-curve pattern. They rise, plateau, and then begin to slide. Another release can fire them up again. Or maybe not.

Then there are the seasonal fluctuations. Summer sales are lesser than winter sales. Holidays may or may not fall equally over the testing periods.

Also, a book can move high on the also-boughts of another book, and then that book can get a spike via a promo or a new release, thus giving your book a piggyback spike. Conversely, your book could fall off the also-boughts of a bestselling book, and lose visibility as a result. This happens all the time. And you have to multiply that effect out over not just one also-bought carousel, but many.

In addition, you don't know what effect the Amazon recommendation engine is having on your sales. How often are they emailing customers to promote it? Amazon sends millions of such emails daily. But how often do they promote *your* book? And to whom? Is it the first book listed in their email, or the last? These things fluctuate as well, and you have no way to know when they change.

And you probably want to do some promotion yourself. You may run BookBub, Facebook or Amazon ads.

All in all, sales volume is in a constant state of flux for reasons mostly beyond your control and ability to measure.

I've probably missed a few causes of sales fluctuation, but you get the point. Sales go up, and they go down. They slide, and sometimes rise again. Against such a background, you can't accurately test one blurb against another.

Worse, you risk changing a good blurb into a bad blurb based on faulty data.

You can try to refine the above method by using Amazon ads. This has similar issues. If you use category ads, you have no control over where your ad is placed. It could be showing on paperbacks or ebooks. It could be showing on closely targeted or loosely targeted products. It could have different placement on a carousel. It could be on the first carousel or the second one below the reviews. Competitors may raise or reduce bids, or remove ads or start new ones for different books. All of this will (sometimes drastically) influence conversion rates.

It's sometimes said among amateurs that a click is a click is a click. But this is not true, and professional pay-per-click advertisers advise good targeting in order to improve conversion rates. Where (and even when) your ad shows will increase or decrease conversions, and testing different blurbs will give you a dog's breakfast for data.

You can try to refine with Sponsored Product ads, which give better targeting. But they still include many of the variables above that invalidate data. Not to mention, because these ads are lower volume, you're not likely to get enough data anyway.

This isn't the place for a discussion of Amazon ads, so I've been extremely brief here. Book three in this series will tell you more than you ever wanted to know about the subject.

It's not that I don't like the idea of testing blurb performance. I love it. *I want it bad.*

But facts are facts. There's no dependable way to test at the moment. I'm not going to waste my time calculating rolling averages against unreliable data. That's time I can better spend by honing my craft (in copywriting and in fiction) and writing more books.

If you're convinced that rolling averages work, and you want to test your blurbs that way, I won't try to talk you out of it. The choice is always yours. But I hope I've prompted you to consider some of the underlying issues that you need to somehow factor in first (if you can find a way) before you try to judge blurb performance on that basis.

16. Feedback Pitfalls

If you can't rely on blurb testing in the marketplace, what *can* you rely on?

The other option available is to get feedback from fellow writers. This is actually quite easy to do. There are several sites where people gather for that purpose. This includes my own Facebook group, which you may already be part of if you've read other books in this series. If not, the details are presented at the end of this book.

The problem with feedback from other writers is that they may or may not be familiar with your genre. This makes a *massive* difference. Also, they may or may not have copywriting skills. Anyone can *say* they're a copywriter. Some people do, even though they've never earned a cent professionally by using copywriting skills. And of course, anyone can give an opinion on a blurb.

But whose opinions should you believe? When should you listen to them and when should you disregard what they say?

What I've tried to do in this book is give you a comprehensive and advanced knowledge of copywriting as it applies to book blurbs. But just as much, I've tried to encourage you to Google your own information and seek confirmation of what I say. By doing this, you'll see the same arguments as I've made, but presented in different ways. This gives you better context. It also deepens your knowledge.

And knowledge is the key here. When you get feedback, you must weigh it against *your* knowledge. Does the feedback display a proper understanding of copywriting principles? If it does, you can rate that feedback more highly. If not, you can rate that feedback less highly.

If you don't understand true copywriting principles, you're working in the dark and can be led blindly one way or the other to no benefit.

So this is my advice. Study this book. Test what I say against what Professor Google says. Then test both against what you see in the marketplace on the bestseller lists. Look for the patterns of confirmation. With a firm idea in your head about how good blurbs work, put your own out there in multiple Facebook groups to get feedback. Feel free to join mine as well for comments. I'd like to see you there.

Then sit back and cherry-pick the best of the advice.

I'd also advise you to offer your own feedback to others. This is one of the best ways to sharpen your skills. Problems in other people's blurbs are more obvious than problems in your own. Helping them helps you, in the long run.

17. Seek Patterns and Discard One-offs

I mentioned patterns just before. Patterns are critical. They let you know when you're onto a good thing, and the lack of a pattern is a warning sign. It might mean you've discovered something new, at least for blurbs, and I never want you to ignore that possibility. But for the most part … it means the idea is a dud.

Here's an example of the sort of thing that can prove misleading, and why you need to dig for the truth to find the patterns of confirmation.

In 1977, Ellen Langer (Professor of Psychology at Harvard) published a study. Her experiment went like this. People were in a queue waiting to use a photocopier. A person attempted to queue jump. At different times, three different wordings were used.

Excuse me. I have 5 pages. May I use the xerox machine?

Excuse me. I have 5 pages. May I use the xerox machine, because I have to make copies?

Excuse me. I have 5 pages. May I use the xerox machine, because I'm in a rush?

The compliance rate to the request was as follows, in the same order as the questions. 60%, 93% and 94%.

Well, that's an interesting experiment. And the conclusion? Just including the word "because" increased compliance rates, and it didn't even need a good reason attached to it to work.

Brilliant. Awesome. We now know that using the word "because" in copy such as blurbs will increase conversion rates. In fact, it's a trend lately in a certain circle to finish blurbs off with a "You'll love this book because" sentence. "Because" is a power word! Time to break out the champers and celebrate. Except…

Not so fast, grasshopper. Never so fast. If I'm teaching you anything in this series it's to dig deeper for the truth.

This is where some professional copywriting background comes in handy. How should that experiment *really* be interpreted? And did Langer herself attribute the results to the word "because"?

First up, there are a few issues with the experiment, at least in terms of blurb effectiveness over 40 years later.

The experiment was done on the basis of queue jumping and not a buy/not buy decision based off a blurb. Those things are as far away from each other as injecting a bodybuilder with mouse steroids on the principle that what works for rodents works for people.

Yikes! Pass the cheese, please.

To my knowledge, no one has conducted split testing on the word "because" in blurbs. Not in a scientifically acceptable way. Refer to the problems associated with attempting to do so outlined in the previous chapter.

But there are other problems with that study. It's old. So old, in fact, that it pretty much predates the digital age. People in a queue are not anonymous finger clickers on Amazon. Might not social cues and a sense of courtesy and manners play out differently 40 years ago, in person, compared to anonymous users on the present-day internet? I'd suggest that's likely. The internet isn't renowned for high levels of courtesy…

There's also limited data. The experiment only included 120 people – it's not statistically relevant.

But, in those famous marketing words – wait, there's more.

Studies can say anything. So can statistics. This is why you dig deeper, research, and look for confirming patterns – if they exist.

As it happens, there's been another study that has bearing on the subject.

Psychologist Stanley Milgram carried out an experiment in the New York City Subway, also during the 1970s.

In short, it went like this. Experimenters boarded busy trains and asked already sitting passengers to give up their seats for them. There were two variations of the request.

Excuse me. May I please have your seat?

Excuse me. May I please have your seat? I can't read my book standing up.

Sound familiar? It's almost the same as the Langer experiment. Something is asked without a reason given, and something is asked with a justification. The only difference is in syntax. "Because" wasn't inserted.

These were the results. For request one, 56% of people gave up their seats. For request two, only 37.2% of people gave up their seats.

In contrast to the photocopier experiment, adding a reason for the request resulted in *fewer* people complying.

How are we to interpret this? Does it all hinge on the word *because*? Is it really a magic word? Or does it all hinge on offering a justification, however sketchy? If so, why do the two experiments give opposite results?

It's worth noting that the original photocopier experiment did *not* give credit to the word "because". This is the name of the paper if you want to research the actual source material. *The Mindlessness of Ostensibly Thoughtful Action: The Role of "Placebic" Information in Interpersonal Interaction.*

That's quite a mouthful. But if you read it, the hypothesis tested and confirmed by the results was that people operate much of the time on a "mindlessness" basis.

This isn't as insulting as it sounds. It just means that people use subconscious rules of thumb to make many decisions. There are rules of thumb on how to behave in many, many social environments, like waiting in a queue or sitting on a train. (See book one in this series for more on rules of thumb in relation to general book-buying decisions.)

The subway experiment was founded on the same hypothesis. That hypothesis suggests that unless the wording of the request jolts someone out of "mindlessness" decisions tend to be processed more or less automatically. If the wording does jolt them, then an actual decision is made and the reason for the request is consciously evaluated and becomes far more important.

This is why the two experiments have opposite results, but still prove the same thing. The rules of thumb for sitting on a train are different from the rules of thumb for waiting in a queue. And the unusualness of a request for someone to take another person's seat on a train prompts a *conscious* decision. The results become even worse when no good reason is given. It's not the specific wording that counts. What counts is the reason. Does it slide under the radar, and go through an unconscious rule of thumb process? Or does it provoke conscious scrutiny? If so, it better be a darn good one.

So the studies have nothing to do with the word "because". They're all about rule-of-thumb decision-making and what wording (justifying an action) prompts a flip to a conscious and scrutinizing decision.

The truth is that "because" is not a power word at all. Although you may hear it called that in a few blogs, even some from copywriters. I think they'd change their mind though if they read the actual study. Most likely few ever have. They picked it up from an influential author called Robert Cialdini, who interpreted (as I think I've shown) the original study incorrectly. This is why it's important to always dig for the truth. *Never take anything at face value.* Question it. If possible, go back to the source.

The point of this longwinded example is that one-offs don't prove anything. Better to look for the patterns. That will give you true confidence in the technique. A few blog posts here and there and a book or two aren't enough. Dig deeper. Seek out the truth. Are copywriters in widespread agreement about a technique? Do you see the tactic frequently at play in advertising?

Let's take this back to blurbs.

Do you really need to give prospects a justification to buy your book? This smacks of trying to overtly convince someone to do something, which is bad copywriting that'll provoke reactance. Especially when the prospect has the time to evaluate your reason. And they will, because using a "buy this book because" formula at the end of the blurb stands out like … dogs' ears.

Far better, in my view, to end with a cliffhanger that makes the prospect yearn to discover what happens next. This is a powerful driving force, and it doesn't require the prospect to think. It can't induce reactance. The prospect instead will operate on the basis of their own personal rule of thumb process for when they love a blurb. For some, that'll be: "Time to check the reviews." For others, it'll be: "Time to check the preview."

And if you do use the "buy this book because" formula, ask yourself what's a more powerful incentive to buy your book. The "because" formula, or the story cliffhanger?

If the formula is stronger, don't you think you need a better cliffhanger?

I've gone into this "because" example in great detail. This is (no pun intended) because it serves as a perfect illustration of the need to dig deeper and verify any technique before you use it. There's a lot of misinformation out there. Misinterpretation is rife. Advice can often be catastrophically bad, no matter that it may come from good intentions

How are you to decide which techniques to use, and which not to use? Especially in a selling environment with so many hidden sales currents, flows and eddies that it invalidates testing?

We can hope that one day Amazon will release to us their data on conversion rates of blurbs. This alone will allow us a reasonably accurate testing of blurb variations. Until then, we have to rely on a fallback option.

Fortunately, it's a pretty good fallback option.

The first step is to understand the theory behind any new technique or tactic. Research it. Evaluate it. Turn it over in your mind. Measure it against what you know of your target audience behavior. Does it seem a good idea?

Step two is to measure it against copywriting practices. Is it a technique that you see in marketing? Do copywriting blogs discuss it? Are they consistent in their advice? Or do some copywriting experts disagree or just omit the technique from their advice?

Lastly, turn to bestselling book blurbs. Do you see the technique at play there?

If all three of these steps show a consistent pattern, then the technique is likely a proven winner. If not, then you likely have a dud.

But, if your gut instinct about a technique is that it will work for you, in your situation and with your voice, then if you have a high risk-tolerance, it might be worth a go. But if another technique is available that does the same job and also passes the three tests, my advice is to use that instead. Only take a risk when there's a large potential gain from it.

A further word now on step three. Most authorities in publishing advise you to look at the blurbs of bestselling books, especially those in your genre. This is consistent with what copywriters do. They always look at the competition and copy from them. In fact, they keep what they call "swipe files" which are collections of good copywriting lifted from other copywriters. Copywriters steal from each other more than Victorian pickpockets used to cut purses.

The advisers who tell you to disregard bestselling blurbs are lone voices. There aren't many of them, and their advice doesn't fit the pattern of what successful authors say (who do advise to study bestselling blurbs). Frankly, the lone voice position is insulting to highly successful authors who've worked very hard to get where they are, and have developed a high-level skillset. They're not consistently on bestseller lists because of luck. They're there because of sweat and correct knowledge. They know stuff, and they network with each other at a high level to pass that knowledge around.

This is not to say that all blurbs on bestsellers are good. Some are shockers. Not all authors are good at blurbs. Not all publishing houses create good blurbs either. For that matter, not all professional copywriters are good, just the same as some bakers or doctors or sports players are better skilled than others.

Fluctuation is normal. Variation causes doubt. So, seek the patterns of success, because they're your life-raft in turbulent seas.

Power words

"Because" is not a power word. Giving a justification is, under certain circumstances, although it carries an equal ability to backfire if misused. But do power words exist?

They do. Copywriters make great use of them. But this is the key, as it is with everything copywriters do. It's not a one-size-fits-all situation. Some words work well on some audiences, but not on others. *Know your audience.*

For book blurbs, this means know your genre and subgenre. Fill your blurb with words that work for them. I don't know what they are for most genres, just like I wouldn't pretend to be an expert in writing blurbs for most genres. You need to live and breathe a particular type of story to know what resonates with the audience for it.

But, by way of example, here are a few of the power words for epic fantasy, in particular old-school epic fantasy. Ancient evil. Emissary of evil. World-spanning. Quest. Dark power. Dark forces. Horde. Sorcery. Final battle. Prophecy. Child of destiny.

What are the power words for *your* genre? Which words are like a seed that's planted in the prospect's mind to grow in their imagination? Because that's how these words work. They're small, but they spark whole vistas of possibility in the reader's consciousness. They bring to life thoughts of other stories that used those same words, and that brings with it the memory of reading pleasure.

That's how those power words work. By association. And it's an incredibly powerful technique. More on that later. There are other power words. Any words that invoke emotion are power words. Risk. Temptation. Danger. Fear. Love. Time is running out. Life-changing struggle. Those are the sorts of words and phrases that I mean.

There's another layer of power words that copywriters use. Words like free, you and discount. But you can only use these types of words when you're talking directly to the reader, and most blurbs don't do that. Most blurbs are a very unusual type of copywriting that comes from the perspective of a character in a story.

But the blurb opening and ending are places where some blurbs do talk directly to the reader. If that's your blurb, it's worthwhile Googling "power words in copywriting" and seeing what turns up that might apply to what you're working on. Treat the lists with a grain of salt though. Some words are much more powerful than others, but a long list looks more authoritative than a short list. And a long list bulks out a blog post nicely too. But never forget that the best and strongest power words are those associated with genre. They beat the others hands down.

A final point. It really goes without saying, but it's easy to fall for the allure of a simplistic approach and believe that just by sprinkling a few power words through a blurb you can transform it into a conversion machine.

It doesn't work that way. Content is king. Use the AIDA formula to give your content a marketing structure. Put the work in to develop multilayered hooks and an emotional connection between character and prospect. That's much harder than throwing in a few power words, but also much more successful. But if you've already done that, then power words are a sweet icing on the cake.

18. Foreshadowing

I touched on this in the last chapter, and earlier in the book as well.

Foreshadowing acts as a kind of shorthand. By invoking words that resonate with a particular genre and have associations with stories that have gone before, and also by hinting at genre tropes, a blurb can say so much more than its mere words allow.

Foreshadowing conjures up a feeling in the prospect of all the things in the story that seem like they will happen, but the blurb need not go to the trouble (and wordage) of trying to explain it. This is a crucial element to blurb writing. Space in blurbs is at a premium, and this technique allows you to do more with less.

Foreshadowing can start up a kind of literary resonance. It's a bouncing around of ideas and it can throw up a whole construct in the prospect's mind. For instance, in epic fantasy the concept of light and dark has been used many, many times to serve as another way of saying good and evil. It gives a sense of opposite forces working at a primal level. It stirs to life dormant memories of the stories of certain authors like Tolkien, Brooks, Eddings and Jordan.

A blurb using the light against dark terminology foreshadows that the story is epic, unfolding on a grand scale. It also connotes a certain mood. It used to be called classic fantasy. Now it's called noblebright fantasy – a direct contrast to grimdark fantasy. I doubt a grimdark story would ever use "light and dark" in either blurb or story itself. Grimdark is all about shades of gray and moral ambiguity.

All this is rather like how a simple smell can trigger childhood memories or suddenly hearing an old song on the radio can take you back to a different time and place. The trigger itself might be small, but the memories and feelings that go with it are vast. Tapping into this in a blurb is a copywriter's dream.

Lest you've begun to believe that I'm making this up, there's a literary term for what I'm talking about. I prefer resonance, but if you want to go all fancy the correct expression is intertextuality. As a literary device, I'm not a fan. As a copywriting technique in blurbs, where the goal is to layer everything so as to increase your bang for buck in limited space, I'm in love. Few things work better in a blurb.

Of course, foreshadowing comes in another form too. In this context, it's just a simple hint of something to come. It doesn't have to resonate with genre on a grand level or anything. It just plants a seed in passing that something is going to happen. It might be as simple as a hint of romance against a backdrop of a thriller. Just keep it to a hint though. It never needs saying outright.

Dropping these little hints saves you the trouble and space of explaining things in detail. And this is where many blurbs go wrong. The more you say about something the more you have to keep explaining it so it all fits together and makes sense. This turns your blurb into a synopsis.

Resist the temptation to explain. Shine a bright light on those few slices of the plot that you've chosen to run with for the blurb, and scatter one or two hints around that foreshadow other story elements. The smaller those hints are, the less you'll feel the need to explain them. But the prospect will pick up on them, and their curiosity will be aroused.

19. When and How to Write the Blurb

It's not my place to tell you when and how to carry out the job. You'll have your own thoughts or routine. But I'll tell you what I do, and why I do it that way.

First, to the when.

I'm an outliner, or a plotter if you like. That means I know where the story is going, more or less, before I've written it. This also means I know the material my blurb can draw on.

I write the blurb after the outline. Sometimes before it, if the story is clear in my head. Doing so gives me the chance to write a first draft of the blurb, and to let it sit for a good while.

I'll return to it periodically while I'm writing the novel. Each time, it has the benefit of being fresh so that I can appraise it better and make improvements. I'll add layers to it. (Yes, I'm a true believer in layering. I think you've noticed that by now.) Each pass is a refinement. And if the story changes, nothing is set in concrete. I can change the blurb too. I'm not chained to my outline.

All this gives me an advantage. When the story is done, and it's gone through its own rewrites, the blurb is ready to go whenever I want to hit the publish button. No last-minute struggle with the blurb for me. It's sitting there, polished and waiting.

I sometimes wonder how many good books get published that took months or years to write, while the blurb was churned out in a mad rush a day before publication. And I also wonder what impact that has on sales.

For myself, I treat blurbs as critical marketing tools. I take my time over them. None is ever perfect. But each one is always much better than it's long-ago first draft.

If you're a pantser (that is, you don't outline and write by the seat of your pants) you don't have the luxury of so much time on the blurb. If that's you, the possibility still remains to write the blurb when you've reached, say, two-thirds through the novel. By then, you know what you need to know for the blurb.

Now, to how.

Again, it's not my place to tell you how to write a blurb. But so many people struggle so hard with it, that I think it's worth sharing this little bit of advice.

Start at the beginning. Sort out your opening first, choosing the best tactic from all those available to you. And then take your cue from that. The tagline, or whatever other method you choose to open, is of immense importance. Get this done first, and get it done to your satisfaction. As a rule of thumb, copywriters will spend as much time on the headline of an ad as on all the rest of the copy combined.

It's of massive importance to start well. But having started, then it's like walking. One step just comes after the next naturally.

You can treat the opening as a springboard. It will launch you into the next phase, but having shaped it so well, it will drive you exactly where you need to go next. If you start a blurb, and then try to fit a tagline to it afterward, it's going to be hard to capture the flow of things. It risks a disconnect between tagline and blurb.

So, my advice is to start from the beginning. Let the first sentence shape the second and so on until you reach your cliffhanger at the end. Go where the blurb takes you, rather than trying to take the blurb where you think best.

Starting with a preconception of what should be in the blurb will only act to stifle your progress.

But at the end of the day, write the blurb when and how you like. If it's working for you, it's working. But if not, try it my way and see if it helps.

I mentioned above that many people struggle with blurbs. They find it easier to write a novel. Well, I think there's a reason for this. You've probably spent years developing your craft as a fiction writer. You know what you're doing. But blurbs are a different animal. You don't have the skillset because you never dreamed of being a copywriter. But once you acquire the skillset and tools of a pro copywriter, all of a sudden blurbs are a joy to write.

I urge you to take the time to develop the skillset. Good copywriting is a lot more like fiction than you may believe. It'll reward you, and when you understand it, it really is a joy to write.

20. The Myth of F-shaped Reading Patterns

The F-shaped reading pattern is a big deal. At least, in copywriting circles, government institutions and among web designers.

It's a big deal because it's true. People scan in an F shape. A picture is worth a thousand words, so I suggest you Google it, and then click the images tab.

Everyone will tell you how important it is. They'll tell you that you need to frontload the interesting bits to headings, first sentences, the opening of sentences...

Sound familiar? We've covered this ground.

But there's one thing left out, and most people don't get it. Especially, government institutions don't get it. I had to do some fast talking in my old job to convince the powers that be.

The F-shaped reading pattern is real, and you should use all the tools at your disposal to combat it. It'll kill your copy *dead* if you don't. (Who says redundancy is bad?)

But the F-shaped reading pattern is also a myth.

How is that possible?

It's possible because most writing fails. Most text *is* read according to the F-shape.

Frontloading helps, but infrared imaging of frontloaded webpages shows the same problem, albeit not as bad. People still scan the pages.

Scan is the relevant word. Scanning is *not* reading. Until people are invested, they scan. It's not worth their bother to read. Reading takes effort.

If you like, frontloading is like the attention phase of the AIDA formula. It's good, but ultimately meaningless unless you work on the next phases of interest and desire.

When people are invested, they read rather than scan. The F shape becomes an E shape. This is what you want.

How do you achieve it?

Don't stop after the frontloading. The second half of a sentence, or the second sentence of a paragraph, is *not* the place to take a breather. This is where most people, even some copywriters, fail. They think they've done the hard work by frontloading.

They haven't. They've only just begun. The trick is to keep the good stuff coming. Effectively, the aim is to try to "frontload" *every* word and phrase. If it's not some kind of hook, if it's not building interest and desire, if it's not signaling genre, if it's not triggering emotions, what's it doing there? Get rid of it.

This is hard. This is very hard. But turning an F into an E is a kind of alchemy. It transforms lead into gold. And by gold, I mean sales dollars.

21. Must a Tagline be 8 Words or Less?

I'll get straight to the point. It's another myth.

What? You want *evidence* for that statement? Excellent! My motto is sinking in. Dig deep. Find the truth. Question standard practice – seek *best* practice. Or, in this case, take nothing at face value. Question everything.

Grasshopper, the student has become the master. But I still know a few things.

One of them is this. Blurbs are copywriting, but not all copywriting is the same. There's no one-size-fits-all approach. Selling lawnmowers has a lot in common with selling books. (Really, it does.) But not everything. And even core incontrovertible principles of copywriting change over time as audiences morph and technology advances.

So, as ever, know your audience.

Where does the commandment for eight word or less (some say six words or less) taglines fit into this?

In ages gone, eight words or less was a thing. But back in the day, magazine copywriters had to worry about brevity because of space concerns. Columns were only so wide, and ads could only be so big. The eight words or less mantra was a layout requirement of the magazine rather than anything to do with copy effectiveness. Let me repeat that. *It was a layout requirement, and nothing to do with the copy.*

Much more recently, studies in the direct mail industry show that 40% to 50% of the most effective headlines are more than eight words.

Bottom line? Take your pick. Long or short is irrelevant. It's the content of the tagline (or opening) that counts.

This is a common theme in indie publishing. People invent rules and say do this or don't do that. Or they borrow rules from elsewhere without an understanding of the background and due thought for if and how it applies to indie publishing. But it all crumbles to dust on research. You can do pretty much anything, so long as you do it well.

There's also plenty of evidence that in a lot of situations long headlines outsell short ones. If you fall for the eight-word rule, you're complying to something established for the magazine industry hundreds of years ago, and it has no bearing on Amazon blurbs in the digital age. Worse, you're depriving yourself of options.

If the best option you have is really short, great. Go for it. But if it's longer, go for that too. Choose what works best for you and your situation.

Are you still choking on what I said just before? *There's evidence that long headlines outsell short ones*. There is. Google "Dan Greenberg neuroscience headline length".

The key points of this neuroscience research are that "native" ads get treated with more respect by a prospect than "foreign" ads. A foreign ad is something like a banner ad that is clearly not part of the real content of the page. It's seen as "other" and for the most part ignored. It's a nuisance, and that's why a lot of people use ad-blockers on their web-browser.

The tagline of a blurb is a natural part of the blurb itself. The prospect expects to see it there. It's not an "ad" at all. This is all the more reason to avoid trying to turn it into an overt ad by having massive fonts at the opening or by placing a buy CTA at the end of the blurb. *Covert marketing works better than overt marketing*. If you turn a blurb into an obvious ad, it'll get treated as such, and you risk it being ignored.

The next part of the research is that certain words grab more attention. These are copywriting power words. And you guessed it – they relate to emotion. Frontload the headline with one or more of these.

Lastly, longer headlines are more effective. Yes. More effective. The longer the headline, the better it engages the client, assuming points one and two are met. Some of the highest-converting headlines on the web are as high as thirty words.

Neuroscience. I love it. It really blows my mind.

22. Blurb Branding

This is by no means a requirement. But it can help.

What's the benefit of it? How does it work?

The best explanation is to look at covers. Most of you will be familiar with branding in that sphere of indie publishing. Covers of a series that look similar are recognizable for just what they are – covers belonging to a series. This helps buyers who may have read earlier books spot a later book when it comes out. Otherwise, it may blend in with a blur of other books and be inadvertently skipped over.

A quick note on branding at this point. What we're talking about here is brand *recognition*. But there are other types of branding, and people lump them together as one. For instance, there's also brand *experience*. Lumping them together is a mistake. They work differently, and have different benefits. If you want to research the subject to verify that I know what I'm talking about (please do – trust no one in this business until you do a *lot* of verifying) Google "benefits of brand recognition".

The question is though, does brand recognition assist blurbs as much as it assists covers?

Not really. By the time the prospect is reading the blurb they probably already know who the author is, and that the book is part of a series they've already started.

Whoops. Go back to that word *probably*. Probably isn't good enough. Probably is vague. Success in this business comes from digging deep to find best practice and getting all the little things right. A lot of little things together add up.

So, while many readers will know exactly what they're reading in this scenario, some won't. They may have clicked on a cover without noticing the author name or series title. Horror of horrors, they may not even remember the author's name, even if they liked earlier books in the series.

This is where blurb branding comes in. It's an additional level of recognition triggering. It will help, some of the time. Do you need it? I'd say no. But that doesn't mean it's not a good idea.

There are lots of ways to brand a blurb. Some are simple, while others are complex.

At the simple level, you can just ensure you have your main character's name right up front. The prospect will remember that better than the author name.

Looking for something more complex? Robert Jordan's *The Wheel of Time* series offers an excellent example. Each blurb starts like this:

The Wheel of Time turns, and Ages come and go, leaving memories that become legend. Legend fades to myth, and even myth is long forgotten when the Age that gave it birth returns again. In the Third Age, an Age of Prophecy, the World and Time themselves hang in the balance. What was, what will be, and what is, may yet fall under the Shadow.

Not bad, eh? You'd struggle to find a better calling card for epic fantasy than that. It speaks to genre, and it has a poetic gravitas. Not to mention a juicy open loop at the end. But it also effectively brands each of the 14 books of the series.

It's not the only series branded like that. For decades, the *Belgariad* series of David Eddings was similarly branded. Why the publishers abandoned it, I don't know. In my view, it was a grave mistake. Evidence enough that the big publishers get things badly wrong from time to time, if you ask me. (This is why you always look for patterns of consistency though.) Anyway, here's how all five book blurbs in the series used to start.

A magnificent epic of immense scope set against a history of seven thousand years of the struggles of gods and kings and men – of strange lands and events – of fate and a prophecy that must be fulfilled!

To my mind, that's even more epic than the previous one. It's a love letter to the genre.

I've picked epic fantasy here because that's the genre I'm most familiar with. What sort of branding occurs in your genre?

The lesson to be learned is that branding your blurbs is something to think about. It may or may not be for you though. It just depends, as always, on your own situation. But if you do it, do it as everything else is done in a blurb – with layering. Speak to genre and include hooks.

23. Difficulties for Later Books in the Series

Is there anything harder than writing a blurb? If there is, it's writing blurbs for follow-up books in the series.

But, as I said earlier, what makes writing blurbs difficult is not having the right skillset. The same applies in this situation.

What's needed here is a blend of two vastly different approaches. It sounds strange, but that's the mindset that works.

The first approach is to treat any blurb for any book as though it's a book one. It's a simple trick, but it'll serve you well. Find your opening, and go from there. Pretend your prospect has never read book one, and write from that perspective.

And guess what? For many people, stumbling across a later book in your series is exactly how they discover you for the first time. If they like what they see there, they go to book one and check you out.

Whatever you do, never assume that the blurb for book two and onwards is only for people who have read book one. That's a mistake that'll cost you sales.

Treat each blurb for every book as though it were book one, and make it as good as you possibly can.

But, and there's always a but, later books in a series will by their nature act as spoilers. For instance, if the hero's life is in jeopardy in book one, the prospect knows he survived the situation if he appears in book two. There's no getting around it.

Authors try hard to though, and they get themselves in a twist trying not to give anything away.

My advice? Don't worry about it.

This is where the second approach comes in. Everything in the modern age of literature is about open loops and posing questions and keeping the audience guessing about what's going to happen next.

But for most of human history the exact opposite was true. Myths, legends, folklore, ballads and stories were all *known* to the audience. When a storyteller held forth on Sigurd the Dragon-slayer, the audience *knew* at the beginning of the tale how it was going to end. The audience of Beowulf *knew* what was going to happen too. The same for stories of Odin and Thor and Achilles and Quetzalcoatl. Or King Arthur.

King Arthur is a good example. The Arthurian Cycle of stories has been going around for well over a thousand years. The core is always the same, it's just the details that change. How many box office hits has King Arthur given Hollywood? When will the next one come out? It won't be too long.

And here's another thing. Why do we reread books and rewatch movies? Clearly, spoilers aren't the deal-breaker they're made out to be.

What counts with this approach is *anticipation*. We know what's coming, and we know we'll like it. We want to relive the joy we had the first time we experienced it. Or, even if we haven't experienced it before, the spoiler whets our appetite anyway. It's an appetizer in the same way that eating food makes you hungry.

This anticipatory approach is immensely powerful. It has a longer history in literature than open loops and teasers. It's hardwired into our brains and our cultural roots. Of the two approaches, it may even be the stronger. I discuss this in more detail, and go into the evidence from neuroscience in book four of this series, which is about general sales copy.

Back to blurbs. The gist of what I'm saying is this. Use open loops, as well as other hooks. Treat any blurb like a book one blurb, except where you can't. Then, if you let loose a spoiler, don't worry about it. It's probably doing you more good than harm. It's really a hook of the fact or statement kind.

Let's turn to movies again. Has there ever been a James Bond film where the suave hero's life wasn't in dire peril? And yet he keeps coming back to the screen, bigger and better than ever. Each exciting car chase, or fight, or hanging-over-a cliff scene is *full* of tension, even though you *know* he's going to make it through.

That's food for thought. That's the anticipatory approach at work.

24. Blurbs and Smartphone Users

Have you ever considered the difference in buyer behavior between smartphone and PC users? Is there one?

Amazon seems to think so.

First, I'm not sure if there are any exact figures for how many people read ebooks on their phone. But it's a lot. The latest data I can find relates to 2015. It was a Nielsen survey that found 54% of e-book buyers read on their smartphone. That was up from 24% in 2012.

What's clear is that a lot of people read on their phones, and the percentage is likely considerably greater now than 54%.

But reading on a phone is not the same as *buying* on a phone. Current statistics for general smartphone online buying (all products, not just books) is that nearly 40% of ecommerce purchases in 2018 were made via a smartphone.

My point?

No one but Amazon knows exactly how many people are buying your books on a smartphone, but it's a lot – and the number is growing. How your blurb performs on a smartphone is critical.

But it's also critical how blurbs perform on a PC. So, before we delve into this, let's establish what the current differences are in the formats and what this says about buyer behavior.

On a smartphone, the right panel of Amazon's product page is gone. This is the buy and give as a gift button etc. Instead, all these features are placed directly below the book image.

The book price, review snapshot etc. remain in a similar position directly below the book cover.

So, effectively, all the same information and features are present, but they've been added in a vertical line rather than horizontally. This has significant impact. On a smartphone, the blurb is *no longer visible* without scrolling down. At least on my smartphone.

This makes a difference. Statistically, fewer people will ever see the blurb. This is just the nature of webpage design. It's the below the fold effect. The moment the prospect actually has to do something, the fewer of them will ever do it.

For these people, they have the option of clicking buy, downloading a sample or looking inside at the preview. I don't see many people buying without checking out the inside of the book, but whether they look inside more or download a sample more, who is to say?

At the end of the day, they'll get to chapter one of your book either way. They just won't have seen your blurb. This is all the more reason (as if there weren't enough reasons already) to make the first sentence of your story rock, and the first paragraph and the first page. It's taking the place of the blurb to sell the book.

The good news is that just as behavioral insights can help blurbs to move people along the sales funnel, they can also be used *inside* the story itself to sell it. That will be the topic of a later book in this series.

Of course, a lot of people *will* scroll down to the blurb. What differences do we see here on a smartphone?

The first is this. The "Read more" CTA is gone. The blurb appears in all its glory.

What impact does this have? The prospect still has to scroll to see all the blurb, so probably not a lot. But scrolling something tantalizingly visible is more likely than clicking a CTA that hides the rest of the blurb behind a wall. I would think that once a prospect gets to a blurb on a smartphone, read through rates go up. Slightly.

Making it harder to see the blurb in the first place reduces its effectiveness, but having got there, scrolling increases read through and *improves* effectiveness. It balances itself out.

What doesn't get balanced out is this, and it's the major difference between blurbs on a smartphone compared to a PC.

Weird spacing. Smartphones have a narrow screen, at least relative to a tablet or a PC. This has a troublesome impact on formatting. Even just a single long word, or two words joined by an em dash, can throw things out and a huge gap can appear within a line of text.

I find it disturbing, but then again I'm not used to it. I'm not a smartphone book reader. Probably those who are have become used to it, because the same problem persists through the text of the book as it does in the blurb.

But there's that word again. Probably. Maybe they *are* used to it, and maybe they just don't care, but still we know that first impressions count. We know the halo effect is a thing, and harnessing its power increases sales.

The remedy to all this is to avoid long words in your blurb, at least as much as possible. This is something you should be doing anyway for readability reasons. Note, I don't mean dumbing things down. I just mean increasing readability. They're not the same thing.

You can check your blurb on your own phone if you have the Microsoft Office mobile app. It's worth doing.

There are alternatives. You can load the blurb into a draft manuscript when you upload the book on the KDP dashboard and check it out in the phone preview. Or, you can take your chances and wait until its published and then just have a look at the product page on your phone.

One further note on this topic. More people are reading and buying on their phones than ever before. Don't ignore the situation just because you compose and upload your books on a PC. Always think of your audience before yourself.

It's worth your while to check how your blurbs look on a phone and what web page design Amazon (or any retailer) is using. The way I've described it here is the way it appears on Amazon now. In a year, who knows what changes they'll introduce? Or, for that matter, if those changes will impact best practice for writing blurbs.

Keep an eye on things. The only true status quo is that the status quo changes.

25. Deconstructing One of the All-time Greats

What follows is a blurb to a book for one of the great bestselling authors in fantasy. David Gemmell. He wrote heroic fantasy, and he did it with character and style.

He's better known in the UK than the US, but his many, many books were bestsellers internationally. I've picked this blurb for a reason. It's one of my favorites.

This is important. When analyzing a blurb, you have to consider two separate issues. First, whether or not you like it. This is simply a matter of taste. It's also a key reason why some people will look at the blurb of a bestselling book, dislike it, and declare it's bad. Worse, they may even say that blurbs don't impact sales, because if you see a bad blurb on a bestseller how important can they be?

A blurb isn't bad because you don't like it any more than it's good because you do like it. And blurbs are the best marketing tool at your disposal. They form the hub around which all your marketing efforts revolve.

The technical quality of a blurb is a completely separate thing from whether or not you like it. When choosing a book to read, put on your reading glasses. When deciding the technical merits of a blurb, put on your *copywriting* glasses and ignore personal preferences.

The following blurb isn't just a favorite of mine, it's also technically excellent. This is no surprise. Bestselling authors tend to get better attention from publishers than run-of-the-mill authors. That's just the way of the world.

The blurb is for book two in the Waylander series. The book is imaginatively titled *Waylander II*. In this respect, it's the perfect example of what I was talking about earlier. It's for a book two, but it reads like a book one. Except for the one part where it gives away a key plot element of book one.

First, I'll give the blurb in full. Then I'll deconstruct it, in granular detail.

'THE HARD-BITTEN CHAMPION OF BRITTISH HEROIC FANTASY' – Joe Abercrombie.

'HEROISM AND HEARTBREAK … GEMMELL IS ADRENALINE WITH SOUL' – Brent Weeks.

High in the wooded mountains of Skeln, the woodsman, Dakeyras, and his daughter Miriel, live a life of solitude. Unbeknown to them, a group of bloodthirsty warriors stalk the mountains. Men who have never known defeat, to whom revenge and torture are meat and drink. For ten thousand in gold they are eager to kill the woodsman.

Battle-hardened warriors all, they have no fear of this task – but they should have. For Miriel is a woman of fire and iron, skilled with bow and blade, and taught her skills by one of the deadliest warriors of all time…

Her father, Dakeyras, better known as Waylander the Slayer.

I don't like that blurb. I *love* it. But that's irrelevant. All that matters is the copywriting craft that's shaped it, and its appeal to the readers of heroic fantasy that make up its target audience.

First, to the opening. The two quotes are in bold. This draws the attention of a prospect. They're also capitalized. This does the same thing. But nothing is overdone. There are no giant fonts or advertising gimmicks that could stimulate reactance. It's still normal text.

It's worth noting as well that each of the two lines are over eight words in length.

The content of the two quotes is more important. And it's *good* content. The quotes come from two famous bestselling authors within the genre. Remember the BookBub research discussed earlier? It showed that including a quote from a well-known author in the genre increased the average click-through rate by 30.4%. They don't tell us what two such quotes do. I'm going to hypothesize an even greater impact on prospects.

Suffice to say, those quotes are a great opening, and no open loops are in sight.

But that doesn't mean different types of hooks aren't layered in there. They're of the statement kind, and tell the prospect in no uncertain terms the genre. *Heroic fantasy* and *heroism and heartbreak*.

But there's a third layer yet — emotional trigger words. *Hard-bitten. Heartbreak. Adrenaline. Soul.* Hard-bitten may seem the weakest, but it's very genre relevant. Heroic fantasy isn't quite grimdark, but there are certainly grim elements to it.

Is there more? Yes. There's also alliteration. Hard/heroic/heroism/heartbreak. Not to mention bitten/British/break.

That opening, as all openings should try to do, works at multiple levels at the same time.

Let's turn to the first sentence after the opening.

High in the wooded mountains of Skeln, the woodsman, Dakeyras, and his daughter Miriel, live a life of solitude.

There's not a lot going on there. But, in short order, it does give us the two main characters of the story. And it

130

establishes setting. This is genre relevant. It's a trope to start the story off in an idyllic rural environment. Tolkien starts in the Shire. Terry Brooks in Shady Vale. David Eddings in Faldor's farm and so on.

The idyllic setting also works to power-up the contrast with the killers who'll be introduced shortly, and it shows us the first part of the stakes. The status quo.

All in all, for a sentence that doesn't seem to have a lot going on in it, it does alright for itself.

Unbeknown to them, a group of bloodthirsty warriors stalk the mountains. Men who have never known defeat, to whom revenge and torture are meat and drink. For ten thousand in gold they are eager to kill the woodsman.

It doesn't take long for us to discover the conflict in the story (or at least the aspect shown in this slice of the plot). And we know these new introductions as the bad guys from the outset. Here again, we have emotional power words. Bloodthirsty. Stalk. Revenge. Torture. Kill.

We also discover the full stakes of the plot. The woodsman's life, and by extension his daughter's. And a sharp contrast is established between the good guys – the woodsman and his daughter – versus the bloodthirsty warriors, to whom revenge and torture are meat and drink.

But we learn more. The woodsman and his daughter are alone. But they're hunted by a "group" of warriors. That is, they're outnumbered. And the men in that group have "never known defeat". This means the odds are in favor of the bad guys. By a lot. This invokes sympathy for the woodsman and his daughter. It also poses a hook. How are they going to get out of this situation? Is it even possible?

There's another hook too. *Ten thousand in gold.* Who is paying this? Why? It's a lot of money to kill a simple woodsman. So, evidently, there's more going on than we can see. But this is the only hint of it. Nothing else is said, and no explanation is given.

A lesser blurb writer *would* have tried to offer some sort of explanation. If the blurb were placed up on an internet forum, people would say that information needed context.

But the blurb writer knew what he was doing. He dropped a hint, foreshadowing more, and then moved on. Less is more.

Battle-hardened warriors all, they have no fear of this task – but they should have. For Miriel is a woman of fire and iron, skilled with bow and blade, and taught her skills by one of the deadliest warriors of all time…

Just when we think we know what's going on – a twist. This Miriel is a whole lot of woman. The stakes can't really get any higher. It was already a matter of life and death. But now we know, unexpectedly, that those stakes are going to be contested hotly. And by an admirable woman. I say admirable, but I might as well say *likeable*. We like those we admire.

This paragraph nicely sets a hook too. She was *taught her skills by one of the deadliest warriors of all time…*

Who was that? Why did he teach her? Why did she want (or need) to learn? And the ellipsis works with it to add force to the idea that there's a lot more going on that we just don't know about.

We also have in this paragraph an appeal to female demographics. Miriel is a strong female character. This adds depth to what we would otherwise have, which was generally for a male demographic revolving around warriors and fighting.

Her father, Dakeyras, better known as Waylander the Slayer.

Oh my! Another twist. Miriel's father, the seemingly simple woodsman, is one of the deadliest warriors of all time? He was the one who taught her how to fight?

That's unexpected. It also makes you reevaluate what's about to go down. The woodsman and his daughter are outnumbered by men who have never known defeat, but boy oh boy, this faceoff is gonna be big. Someone get the popcorn. All hell is about to break loose.

Revealing the woodsman's former identity is a spoiler too. It is for book two, but also for book one. His life is in jeopardy in book one.

Also, there's another hook. The woodsman and his daughter are the good guys. But Waylander the Slayer doesn't sound like the nice guy living over the road that you wave to when going to the shops. How did the woodsman gain such a name? Is he a good guy or a bad guy? Whatever his history is, it sure must be complex. And interesting.

Right. We've reached the end of the blurb, but we're not done yet. I have some general comments.

That blurb is simple and clear. There are hints of unexplained things going on, but that doesn't prevent an easy read from the first word to the last. Aiding this is a Flesch-Kincaid score of 69. I'd prefer it a little higher than that, but it's still in the high-readability zone. The blurb also comes in at 126 words. Perfect.

The other factor in its readability is that it keeps things simple. We only have four proper names, so there's no name soup. And there's no plot soup either. The blurb serves us up only a tiny slice of the plot pie, but one that represents genre. What's described is basically just the opening of the book (but the plot slice could have come from anywhere else too).

Let's turn to the language of the blurb. Its diction is terse and poetic. It's not quite "high style" but it's approaching it. It's representative for the genre. It speaks with the voice of heroic and epic fantasy. But the plot details narrow it down to heroic fantasy.

Poetic? Yes indeed. This is its voice. It's peppered with alliteration. Wooded. Woodsman. Warriors. Mountains. Miriel. Men. Meat. Skeln. Stalk. Solitude. Dakeyras. Daughter. Defeat. Drink. Live. Life. Unbeknown. Bloodthirsty. Battle-hardened. Bow. Blade. Torture. Ten. Group. Gold.

You'll get a better sense of alliteration in the blurb by reading through it again, picking those sounds out. But the poetry isn't just from the alliteration.

Men who have never known defeat, to whom revenge and torture are meat and drink.

This isn't normal prose. There's alliteration, but mostly the meat and drink bit are strong metaphors. And they tie in with the earlier "bloodthirsty".

For Miriel is a woman of fire and iron, skilled with bow and blade, and taught her skills by one of the deadliest warriors of all time…

Again, there's alliteration here. And again, metaphor. Miriel isn't really made of fire and iron. Also, I would classify this as elevated diction.

So, there you have it. This, I think, is a great blurb. Truly brilliant. Not just to my taste (though it is) but at a technical copywriting level.

Is it perfect? Hells no. No blurb ever is. The main fault to me is that it doesn't mention magic. Magic is an inherent part of the genre, and the blurb should signal that.

Your aim, in writing a blurb, is to get it as close to perfect as you know how. Never settle for close enough is good enough. But at the same time, you can only do so much. Spend a lot of time learning the art of blurb writing, but don't become obsessed by it.

At least, if you can stop yourself. In its way, copywriting is as alluring as writing fiction. If you have the bug you can't stop.

26. The HOOKER Method™

I like to give people options. This book has been a comprehensive guide to copywriting for blurbs. But, after helping a legion of authors in my Facebook group, I know some people just want a quick and easy formula they can call to mind when writing a blurb.

Here it is. I call it The HOOKER Method™ of blurb writing. You won't forget the acronym, so half the battle is won right there.

Don't be deceived by the name or the simplicity of it. This formula is based on years of copywriting experience, my career as a fulltime author and helping all those authors write better blurbs.

Here it is.

HOOK the reader from the first words

OMIT needless plot

OPEN LOOPS at the ends of paragraphs pull readers forward

KEEP it simple, clear and logical

END with escalating stakes and a cliffhanger

REFERENCE genre tropes throughout

Hooking the reader right from the beginning is vital. More people stop reading at the opening than at any other point. Get more to the end, and your sales will increase. Whether you open with a tagline, review quote or accolade your first words function like the headline of an ad. And on average, only two people out of ten read past the headline. But if your hook performs better than the average, you just gained an advantage over your competition.

Omitting plot stops the blurb from turning into an outline. Pick just a few strands of your story that represent the genre. You don't want to convey the story of the whole book. You want to show the reader snatches of it so they get a feel for what it's like. That's all they need. More just dulls the appetite like eating dessert before dinner.

Open loops are teasers. Paragraph breaks are a natural stopping point where people tend to lose interest and stop reading. Mini teasers at just that moment pull them onward like a kitten chasing a laser light on the carpet. It's a cheap trick, but it works.

Keeping things clear is critical. In copywriting, the saying goes that "confusion kills sales." Reverse gear here, and use clarity to drive conversions.

Ending on escalating stakes and a cliffhanger twines tension and curiosity to ratchet up interest. It's like pouring petrol on a fire from one side and blowing oxygen from the other. They feed each other and entice readers to the reviews or preview. Surveys show that between 60% to 90% of people look at reviews as part of their online buying decision. Add on people looking at the preview, and it's clear that the end of the blurb isn't where people buy. So avoid "Buy now!" calls to action here when the reader isn't ready to purchase. Does "Buy now!" work on you, anyway?

Referencing genre tropes triggers the emotions of the reader. They act as signposts saying what sort of things are inside the book that they like to read. A scattering of the right words and themes foreshadow the entire world of the book to them.

There you go. The HOOKER Method™ is the baby steps approach. It'll work wonders though. Unlike other blurb formulas, it's constructed to harmonize with the sales funnel and the neuroscience of persuasion.

For those who want an elite-level overview of blurb writing however, the next chapter is for you.

27. A Blurb Master Checklist

I've called this a checklist, but I'm not happy with that. It's the best word I can think of though. It's most certainly not a cheat-sheet. There's no substitute for actually knowing and understanding the detail of all the subjects covered in this book. In depth.

What *is* this list then? Think of it as a memory aid like The Hooker Method™, only more advanced and complex.

But, please remember what I said earlier. No blurb is perfect. No blurb will have all the things layered into it that I mention here. But the more the better. Aim for perfection, and see where you land. It will take you further than aiming for mediocrity. Every time.

Here we go:

Know your audience. Understand general reader behavior and also subgenre expectations.

Work to the AIDA concept, which taps into buyer psychology at different stages of the sales funnel.

Pick your best opening after considering all the options available to you. It'll be a hook of one of the various kinds, (fact, statement, open loop, say whaaat, poetic, contrast, direct question, story quote, review quote, award or accolade, referencing other authors or even a standard paragraph). But layer it with other hooks.

Keep in mind the benefits of the halo effect.

Don't be constrained by an eight word or less opening limit. If it's good, longer is *better*. Use the length that works best for your blurb.

Slip in words that evoke emotion. Spark up those mirror neurons.

Slip in words and situations that resonate with the subgenre, and (if possible) the classics of the subgenre (intertextuality).

Frontload. On a PC, there's an above the fold area. Use it wisely. You want copywriting to do its job. Utilize this space. Words sell, not emptiness. But keep it balanced. A wall of text is no good either.

Frontloading isn't enough. Make every word, phrase and sentence count. There's no place to take a breather.

Introduce only a slice of the plot pie. Pick a slice (or a few slivers) that represent genre. Let the prospect get to know your main character and develop rapport.

Keep slipping in hooks and emotional and genre-relevant words.

Build sympathy for your main character. I don't mean empathy, although that's good too. I mean sympathy. It's blurb rocket fuel.

Note where the natural stopping points are. Insert hooks there. Think of a net now instead of hooks. Capture as many prospects as possible. Pull them through the blurb.

Insert appeals to different (but only if appropriate) demographics. Think male and female. Character and plot. Action and emotion.

Ensure there's some kind of goal. Give the hero something to strive for, and the prospect someone to like and cheer for.

Ensure there's an opposing force. This builds tension.

Toward the end, raise the stakes. A love interest, ticking clock etc.

Toward the end, introduce a twist.

Write with clarity. Avoid name soup and plot soup. Keep cause and effect in the right order.

Write with voice. But *not* editor's voice. Don't sound like ten thousand other blurbs.

Foreshadow with hints. Don't explain them.

Make the blurb long enough to take a prospect through the phases of attention, interest, desire and action. But no longer.

Plug any gaps and turn the F-shaped scanning pattern into an E-shaped reading pattern.

Consider how your blurb works on a smartphone.

Avoid a buy or similar CTA. End with a cliffhanger to drive people farther along the sales funnel to the reviews or preview.

Review for phraseology that may cause reactance, and remove.

There you have it. That brings all the concepts together. But success lies in the nuances, and I reiterate that this is only meant as a memory aid and not a substitute for an in-depth understanding.

28. A Facebook Group to Seek out Best Practice

We've covered a lot of ground together. But at the beating heart of this book has always been one guiding belief: success stems from questioning standard advice and striving for best practice.

And best practice, like the truth, is out there. But no one person understands it all. Still less do people share. When they discover a nugget of gold, they tend to keep it to themselves.

But there's another way. Often writers *do* share. I've been fortunate in my writing career, and I've come across a number of people like that. I've benefited from their generosity. They're one of the reasons I can write for a living. With this in mind, I've started a Facebook group in that spirit. Its name?

Author Unleashed

Join me there. It's closing in on 2,000 members. Many are bestsellers. Some are Top 100 sellers. There are some famous indie names in that group, and they share their knowledge. Our motto is this: Dig deep. Find the truth. Question standard practice – seek *best* practice. We're a group that shares knowledge freely. It's a place to get feedback on blurbs and Amazon ads until they're honed to razor-like effectiveness. It's a place to discuss, discover and even drive the cutting edge of marketing for authors.

Want to be part of that? I look forward to meeting you.

Here we are. At the end.

I've talked a lot about business in this book. It is, after all, a marketing book. I've used terms such as "prospect" instead of "reader". But don't let that mislead you. I'm an artist. I love nothing more than to paint a picture with words. I think there's no nobler art than that of the storyteller.

But this book will be judged on its merits. It'll be judged by how well it did its job of giving you, the reader, information to help you on your writer's journey.

What I *hate* after reading a book like this is the feeling that it was stuffed with irrelevant and useless padding. What I *hate* is if the information I paid for was easily available elsewhere on blogs and the like.

If I've done those things to you, I deserve a review bomb.

On the other hand, if I've filled each chapter with good information that'll help your blurb writing, and I've given you a perspective on things that you haven't seen elsewhere, and most especially, if I've given you correct knowledge that will guide your labor, then I'd like to know that. Tell me in the reviews on Amazon. Tell me if this is a good book. Did I live up to my goal of giving you the *definitive* guide?

What the experts say is that I'm supposed to insert a link here to make it easy for you to leave a review. They're not wrong. But I'm not going to do that. You know how to leave one if I've helped you.

The choice, as always, is yours.

I went into a lot of detail on blurbs in this book. Blurbs are critical to publishing success. All roads lead to Rome, and all book marketing leads to the blurb. But you have to drive traffic from *somewhere* first.

Book three in this series, *Amazon Ads Unleashed*, deals with that. As with this book, I leave no stone unturned, and many, many things will surprise you. Amazon ads, done with marketing expertise, can take your publishing to the next level and drive targeted traffic willing to buy at full price. This book will show you how to do that.

Interested?

Thanks for reading. And as always, keep digging for the truth!

Made in the USA
Monee, IL
29 July 2024